Front Porch Talk

*Boone Co. stories I share with
family and friends.*

Johnny

John Edward Jordan Jr.

Copyright © 2016 John Edward Jordan Jr.

All rights reserved.

ISBN: 1530601096
ISBN-13: 978-1530601097

Dedication

Front Porch Talk is a collection of bedtime stories shared with my children. The book is dedicated to my wife, Marian, my family who has always supported my efforts, and to my extended family and friends of Boone County, West Virginia.

Johnny

CONTENTS

Acknowledgments

1   Front Porch Talk June 05, 1955

2   Last Train from Nellis July 25, 1955

3   A Wake on Joe's Creek August 07, 1955

4   Last Steam Engine Through Brushton August 02, 1957

5   Bloomingrose Family Stories August 12, 1957

6   Back Porch Cardinals September 04, 1957

7   Hunting Pa Paws September 28, 1957

8   Parable of the Christian Potatoes October 06, 1957

9   The Missionary's Wife October 20, 1957

10   Wild Ride in Rumble October 26, 1957

11   Trick-or-Treat October 31, 1957

12   Caged Bear at Glasgow November 02, 1957

13   Rocking in the Devil's Chair November 05, 1957

14   Hunting Molly Moochers April 27, 1958

15   Dropline Surprise-Homemade Flies August 14, 1960

16   Peytona Beach June 25, 1961

17   When I First Saw Beauty November 04, 1963

18   Last Wake at Bloomingrose March 25, 1962

Acknowledgements

Front Porch Talk is a companion book of *Ted! It's Too Close Till Sunday* originally collected in the oral tradition of family stories passed down from father to son. My Grandfather Edward Lee Jordan, (Pa Paw Ted), my father, John Edward Jordan, Sr., and my mother, Lucille Midkiff Jordan told stories to entertain me, my brother, Larry, and sister, Michelle in the mountain story telling tradition their parents and grandparents has modeled. I continued in the spoken tradition of spinning tales of Boone County, West Virginia, adventures to our children Trece, John (Buddy), Lee, David, and Logan in the hope of continuing the family's story telling tradition to the next generation. Although, the oral tradition of passing stories, from one listener to another, enables the storyteller to take ownership of the creation, it also provided a large hole capable of swallowing hundred-year-old adventures that would never be repeated at bedtime or before a roaring campfire.

My first attempt of recording our family's stories took the form of letters written home to family and friends. The stories were well received, and often, I have been flattered when visiting Mom and she would show me her drawer of letters. A favorite American History teacher, Jean Vickers Arvon, would flatter me, saying she and Mr. Arvon would often take a letter from her desk drawer and re-read it, and laugh hard, equal to the first reading. Yet, the written record of Jordan, Midkiff, and Hudson family stories remained a fragile record considering the circumstances.

I entertained publishing the letters under the book title, *Letters Home*, but the format was not friendly to unfamiliar readers, and I reviewed a number of letter collections, of famous people, and discovered the reader's interest was mostly spurred by a need for research, and not necessary for pleasure or even as a family keepsake. The writing of letters allowed me to practice telling a story regardless if it was describing a family birthday party, holiday celebration, or describing the excitement we all felt at the birth of a new grandchild, I saw the power of conversation. Before, I was baptized by the spirit of conversation, a typical letter home describing a new birth no differently than a Times-Picayune birth announcement. By utilizing face-to-face conversation, the scene came alive for all readers.

"The baby is crowning!" Dr. Lovejoy cautioned the anxious mother. "Get ready, one more push!"

"Huh!" the first time mother screamed as the baby was cradled by the doctor, and made ready to join his new family.

"You have a fine big boy!" Although the old doctor had made the statement hundreds of time, it was always the best part of his job. "Are you ready to hold your son?" He questioned, following dictated hospital protocol, yet needing no verbal response, seeing the mother's outstretched arms. "I'll go tell your family the good new!" Dr. Lovejoy added, then left the delivery room to share the good news.

Writing is like a mother giving birth, and I have anguished justifying if time spent in my selfish pursuit of hoped acknowledgment measures against lost time with our family. (Time will tell.) A favorite Southeastern Louisiana University professor, Howard Nichols, once mentioned his hardest task, as a writer, was to mark through or discard what he had previously written, and now, I understand his candid confession. I mentioned to Marian, I felt guilty deleting words, sentences, paragraphs, and pages, and wondered if I had condemned them to a state of written word Purgatory. Marian replied, John, I'm worried about you!"

My gratitude continues to be unbounded to Marian, the skinny girl I met at Racine, West Virginia, for her support that enables me to have purpose. I am a hard judge on my accomplishments, much of which I measure as failures, but my greatest triumphs pale, compared to our family, our strength. As with my other publications, incomplete pages would litter my work area without the technical support from our daughter, Trece Jordan-Larsen, and our children: John, Lee, David, and Logan along with daughter-in-laws: Paige White Jordan and Alyssa Markham Jordan, son-in-law: Brian Larsen, Grandchildren: Gage, Cayleigh, Genevieve, Logan Jr., John Harrison, Sarah, Laura, and Julia, and great granddaughters: Violet and Lena.

I am indebted to the kind people of Brushton and of West Virginia that tolerated a rambunctious young boy, always in the center of everyone business. *Ted! It's Too Close Till Sunday* and *Front Porch Talk* both reminded me of the spirit of people gathered on Brushton front porches in the evening time: playing with their children and talking with family and neighbors. Again, Pa Paw Ted will hunt pa paws up Kinder Branch and Dad coal car ride at Rumble, while we go with Mom to visit the "farm," and Aunt Lydia again, feeds the chickens and gather eggs at Bloomingrose.

We'll always enjoy Ma Maw Oma's fried chicken at Sunday dinner after she gives thanks. "Dear Heavenly Father. Thank you for all our blessing you give us. Continue to look after our family and friends. In Jesus' name. Amen."

Chapter 1
Front Porch Talk

"Lenor ran out of the house with just the clothes on her back. She shooed the children up the hill, and the river water was knee deep when they passed through the gate." Grandpa Hudson said while leaning back in the porch glider, then stood and tapped his pipe against his hand to empty the burned tobacco.

"Grandpa, what happened next?" I inquired. It was a typical dinner after Sunday services at the Brushton Methodist Church of fried chicken and mashed potatoes served in the dining room. Later, the group relaxed on the front porch, but it was a special day since Uncle Ira Price, Grandma Hudson's brother, and his wife, Aunt Mary, came for a Sunday visit from Concord, West Virginia, upriver above Whitesville. Uncle Ira and Aunt Mary were as different as day and night. He was a massive man and she was petite; he was loud and she was quiet. Everyone looked forward to their visits. Uncle Ira at one time was a deputy sheriff, and Dad often referred to the stories he told twenty years before on the front porch. According to Uncle Ira, he had captured villains ranging from bank robbers to truant student.

"Uncle Ira, how did you lose your fingers?" I asked, since never seeing someone's missing fingers, and everyone mentioned the missing fingers when talking about him.

"Now, Johnny, Uncle Ira doesn't want to talk about his accident!" Ma Maw Oma shushed me, hoping she could end the embarrassing situation.

Uncle Ira enjoyed repeating the story, "Well, Johnny, I lost my two fingers at the Red Parrot," he raised his left hand to show his missing fingers.

"A red parrot ate your fingers?" I asked wondering why anyone would have a finger eating bird.

"The Red Parrot was the name of a coal company, and the parrot that took my fingers was a conveyor belt," he added and then laughed.

"Did you bring your fingers home and have them in a jar like Sister Rogers' gallstones?"

"No! My fingers were carried on down the belt, through the processing plant, and dumped in a coal car. Guess it was better than if I had lost my fingers in a pickle factory, and they would have been found in a pickle jar at your Grandpa Hudson's store."

Grandpa Hudson was quick to change the subject away from fingers in a pickle jar to a safe subject. "We were lucky our house and the store building wasn't washed down the river like the Peytona Baptist Church and a lot of other buildings," Grandpa finished and relit his pipe.

"Grandpa what happened next?" I asked while Ma Maw Oma brought out homemade apple pie made with Grandma Hudson's June apples with a side serving of vanilla ice cream. The ice cream was store bought, but on special occasions, like the 4th of July, Pa Paw and I worked on their little back porch, turning the crank to make our own ice cream. Everyone was so satisfied with vanilla no one considered another favor.

"Uncle Ira, the apples are from Mommy's trees,"

Ma Maw noted, bring attention to Mommy's apples and Ma Maw's pie. The Hudson home place was on a rise of land between the Hudson Brothers store building and the Brushton Methodist Church. Before Grandpa build their home, a log cabin stood on the hilltop, and the houseless sandy soil of Brushton was planted in tobacco. The C&O track skirted the front, making a steep incline covered with vines of honeysuckle. Beyond the track, a row of small three-room houses lined the river's floodplain and were victims during the annual spring flood.

"Lenor always teased Reginald that she had found him after the flood, being born eleven days after the wash-out," Grandpa laughed and continued his story of the great flood. "Peytona couldn't recover after the cloudburst, and we moved downriver to Brushton." Grandpa Hudson again stood to empty his pipe while looking down over the little town of Brushton that he and his brother, Alonzo, (Uncle Lon) built to support their general merchandise store.

From the front porch, Grandpa Hudson viewed the two-story brick store building and the trackside row of houses he rented to families, the same families had lived in for decades. All the houses had full-length front porches that served as an outdoor room for family gatherings on summer evenings and on warm Sunday afternoons. People took pride in their front porches, always having a fresh throw-rug to welcome muddy shoes, which was a constant presence on the dirt streets. Ma Maw always had an array of potted plants of petunia, impatient, and geraniums; it was a spring tradition to take Ma Maw to the Kanawha City nursery to buy plants. Pa Paw and I always followed up with a Saturday afternoon visit up Kinder's Branch, where we collected rich soil where a 19th century saw mill once was located, and its sawdust had rotted and turned into rich soil. When Pa Paw passed, Ma Maw would declare, quit firmly, "I want nothing alive around me!" In the spring, Mom continued to take her to buy potted plants, and I guess Ma Maw's declaration was an expression of mourning for her loss.

Grandma Hudson took pride looking over Brushton during the spring, the white blooms of her apple orchard, and during the summer, the glistening leaves of Silver Maples trees marked corner boundaries of every front yard. When the wind blew, leafs turned to revile a silver bottom side against a dark green top, and from her front porch it was a lovely view. Ma Maw Oma said her mother planted each Silver Maple and watered them until they took root in the sandy soil of Brushton. After the trees matured, Grandma Hudson was the sole Silver Maple tree lover, since their canopies was thick with leaves, the first to fall in the autumn, roots that broke the ground making grass mowing nearly impossible. An extensive root system raised sidewalks and snaked into sewers, and when traveling under houses, they sprouted, resulting in a jungle of growth.

"John, how high did the flood water get in Brushton?" Uncle Ira asked. Everyone called Grandpa Hudson "Mr. Hudson," but being a brother-in-law and the same age his greeting was unique. Pa Paw always called Grandpa "Mr. Hudson" and when speaking of his to me referred to his as "Grandpa Hudson."

"Ira, a tree was marked; water was at least five feet at the store location," Grandpa Hudson reported. The flood of August 09, 1916 was a paramount event to the people living on Big Coal River. Old people talked of it like it was an event that occurred last summer; it still haunted them nearly fifty years later. At Bloomingrose, the flood was still reverent; Aunt Lydia repeated the story when she was fifteen, sewing on the upstairs porch early the morning of the flood and hearing the river rushing. Her sister, Esther, a school teacher, returned from up the road after being blocked by high water. The family had no time to gather belongings and escaped to the safety of the hillside, while her father was wading waist-deep water in an attempt to store belongings upstairs. Unlike the Hudson family at Peytona, the family's store building was washed away, but their house remained even though water was sixteen inches on the second floor. Grandma Edna's sister, Hazel, spotted the Midkiff store building floating down river above Peytona and canned goods spilling from shelves through a missing wall.

    Old people referred to the August flood as a cloudburst up on Pond Fork, likely the remnants of a tropical depression that stalled over the area. The forest that had once protected the valley from fast runoff had been clear-cut by timber company of the late 19th and early 20th century. The timber industry was coming to an end in Boone County by this time, as evidenced when the large Lackawanna lumber mill at Seth washed out with the great flood, the band saw mill was not rebuilt. Locals supplemented family incomes by running small one-man sawmills, often relying upon rough-cut mine support posts, referred to as "poor man's posts," since no one could make a living cutting or selling them to mines.

"Ted! You need to take Johnny for a walk," Ma Maw whispered while pulling her husband to the side, "he's out in the orchard throwing Mommy's apples!"

"Oma, the boys just practicing his pitching when he pitches for the Cardinals!" Pa Paw made an excuse that Ma Maw took no store, since she viewed baseball, just one step above sitting on a stool at the Muddy Duck bar.

"Ted, for the life of me!" Ma Maw using a neutral favorite intensifier to express dissatisfaction. When she needed to call on Jesus' intervention, she'd say "If Jesus terries, Jesus give me strength, and in extreme situations, Jesus have mercy!"

I had no interest in baseball except when playing in the back yard, even though I was built for baseball, being a left-handed pitcher and a right-handed batter, but no one ever encouraged the sport beyond our backyard. Pa Paw's nephew, Earl Jordan, Jr., was known as a local baseball legend but had got a "calling" and became a Methodist preacher. Ma Maw was very proud of Junior and often attended his revivals. Occasionally when coming home from Charleston, after a day of Saturday shopping, we would stop for a visit to Pa Paw's, older brother Earl's home on Ring Fork off Hernshaw. It was always a pleasant visit with Earl, his wife, Effie, their daughter, Naomi, and Junior. Pa Paw bachelor brother, Ernie, was known as a local talented fiddle player for square dances, but he never played for us since such music was likely considered un-church like.

I now wonder if Junior followed the Cardinals in the Sunday sports section or slipped to the back porch to listen to the Cardinals and Orioles. I don't recall their conversations during visits beyond the subject "We're doing fine; how are you all doing?"

Dad followed baseball on the radio and in the newspaper and later on TV. I would go with him to Dartmouth, where he would play ball for a local team while I stood behind the backstop where Dad could keep an eye on me while watching for plays to home base. But my attention was drawn to the old abandon Orlandi coal tipple towards the hillside that straddled the C&O track. Unlike the American Rolling Mill Company (ARMCO) tipple at Nellis that was disassembled soon after its closure, the Orlandi, Rumble, and Ridgeview tipples remained for years after their closure. Locals held the remaining structure of the Ridgeview tipple as a hopeful sign someday the mines would reopen, saying there's still a lot of coal left to mine.

"Johnny let's take a walk. We can go to the Wirehouse."

"I still have a lot of apples to throw!" I said.

"Gather some in the bucket, and Aunt Mary can take some home. It'll be a gift. No one should leave Brushton without some of Mrs. Hudson's apples." He may have been thinking that having a few less apples would mean an earlier end of apple season. Ma Maw Oma was in a tizzy from the first apple bloom, worried a frost would burn the buds, until the last apple was picked. It wasn't a love for apples, but her concern for Grandma Hudson's apple obsession. While watching TV was a sin for Ma Maw, a wasted apple left on the ground was a sin to Grandma Hudson.

We walked upriver, sometimes on the road and sometimes on the rail track. We passed by the small houses by the river where everyone was gathered on their front porches on Sunday afternoon. As we passed, old people strained their eyes to identify the strollers, then called, "Ted, afternoon. Going for a walk?" was the universal call. We would wave to them, and Pa Paw would tell me who they were or something about them. "The Hale's garden sure looks good this year." The old couple resumed their front porch vigil. Mr. Hale sat in his rocker wearing a suit jacket and white shirt buttoned at the top, and Mrs. Hale rocked while wearing a 19th century bonnet used to shield her head and eyes while working in the garden during the early mornings and late afternoons. Other neighbors cultivated front yard gardens to supplement their diet and to have something to do. They rested on their front porches waiting for the cool evening in the garden.

"Pa Paw? Does Ma Maw know we live next to the Hells? She would sure be upset!" I questioned, since schooled early in hell and brimstone.

Pa Paw laughed then explained, "Johnny, that's just their last name, like your name is Jordan."

We continued our walk to the Wirehouse, a location that once served as an industrial and community recreation site, now just a gathering place for locals. Several wood warehouse buildings painted silver remained that once housed drilling equipment and supplies for the Libbey-Owens-Ford gas division. The Big Coal River gas field had been developed to supply natural gas to fuel the glass furnaces at their Kanawha City glass plant established in 1917. Pa Paw worked for the gas division during the 1930s, being one of the few locals to be employed during the Great Depression. He bailed wells to maintain "rock" pressure and flow for wells that often flooded out with water. Ma Maw, Dad, and Pete often took him lunch and pictures of them picnicking with a well head in the background exist. Other men spent their working life employed by the gas division, known for low wages and few benefits. The wirehouse was named because drill cable was stored at the location, where once a rail-side served the site but was now removed. Bricks outlining forgotten flower beds remained, and a brick barbeque pit made of kiln firebricks was still used by local family for cookouts. A swinging bridge connected upper Brushton with Brier Branch, once a small community across the river. Weeds would have long ago reclaimed the Wirehouse if not for the popular swimming hole. An inclined sand beach was on the Brushton side, and deep water fronted the Brier Branch side of the river. The popular swimming hole was second in popularity to Peytona Beach, which had a broad flat beach on both sides and deep water.

"Pa Paw, I'm going to pick some flowers for Mom," I said after seeing come wild flowers peaking from the encroaching weeds.

"Lucille would like some flowers. We need to get back to Brushton before they wilt in the sun."

When we returned, Mom and Dad were on the front porch, and Mom took the flowers to place in a vase of water while Dad and Pa Paw talked.

"Obble, (Pa Paw always called Dad by his pet name while Ma Maw always called him John Edward) are you going back to Marietta, Ohio, soon?" Dad and his brother both traveled out-of-state for work during the 1950s, ranging from Detroit to cities on the Atlantic coast.

"Dad, Pete and I are leaving tonight; sure is a lot closer then Baltimore!" Then Dad continued, and Mom returned to the porch swing. Not much traffic traveled through Brushton on a Sunday afternoon after everyone returned from church. It was an extreme situation when a train passed on Sunday, and movement on the road was restricted to kids walking or riding bikes. In the evening, traffic would increase as a result of seven o'clock evening church service.

"Dad, have you heard about any work in Charleston?"

"Johnny and I stopped by the union hall yesterday and a little job is starting up at the telephone company. Work will start in a week and last at least two weeks." Then he added, "Oma's got a list of projects; she said the front porch needs a fresh coat of paint."

"Ma Maw said, I can help paint the porch. She thinks it's be a blessing to have a bright front porch for the 4th of July," I added.

Chapter 2
Last Train from Nellis

"Pa Paw, what are we going to do at Nellis? I don't need a haircut and it's not Sunday," I, being Johnny, Ted Jordan's grandson, asked as we traveled up Brush Creek towards the ARMCO community of Nellis. The town was a model company town created by the American Rolling Mill Company headquarter at Middletown, Ohio, to mine the Number 2 Gas metallurgical seam of coal that outcropped at the town site. The 1953 Horizon Blue and India Ivory Chevrolet Bel Air slowed at the first of the five C&O Railroad crossings. The rail dominated the valley floor with Brush Creek and a two-lane paved road yielding to the lay of the railroad's right-of-way. It was habit and a cautious response that slowed the car since the unlit railroad crossing signs and a warning blast of a steam whistle or diesel horn were the sole alerts. Train-car collisions were unreported on the dead end spur track to Ridgeview, mainly as a result of the train's slow speed. Residents and drivers in Marmet weren't as fortunate, as highballing freight and passenger trains took a yearly toll regardless of warnings from blasting steam whistles or diesel horns, flashing lights and clanging bells of railroad guards, or the caution of pedestrians and drivers.

"Pa Paw, tell me again about old Mrs. Stone's milk cow that was hit by the train," I begged for a repeat of the story told nearly every trip up Brush Creek when Ma Maw Oma wasn't in the car. "Did old Mrs. Stone's family eat her milk cow?"

"Well it happened just up the track. The Stone family rented an old trackside house and were so poor that for Sunday dinner that all shared one slice of bacon. Mrs. Stone would tie a piece of string onto the one slice of bacon and give it to one of her six children, and it would be swallowed. She'd reel in up with the string and then give it to the next child to swallow and repeat it until the last of her six children had has a taste of bacon."

"You mean they didn't have fried chicken and mashed potatoes for Sunday dinner?" I asked, knowing the answer but eager for a repeat of the story. "Where was her husband?"

"Years ago, he went down to Grandpa Hudson's store at the mouth of John's Hollow to buy a stove pipe and never returned."

"Well, what happen to him? Was he eaten by bears or black panthers?" I inquired.

"Sister Justice was the last to see Rollin Stone when he waved to her from the rear deck of the C&O caboose headed to Brushton," Pa Paw added.

"He was going the wrong way. Grandpa Hudson's store was up the road in the old yellow building. You told me that's where Grandpa was attacked by a band of women robbers. Uncle Jiggs (Reginald Hudson) saved his life and pocket watch when he chased them out the door!" I interjected. "Slow down, so I can see grandpa's old store building."

The car slowed to allow a view of the yellow trackside building that once provided store goods to residents of John's Hollow. It was convenient to have a local store several miles closer than the company store at Nellis, which was known for high prices. Small country stores provided easy access to locals landlocked in their community by the lack of cars and other merchants.

Pa Paw continued, "Rollin was never heard from again. His family lived on commodity cheese, powdered milk, and one slice of bacon on Sunday. The boys hunted squirrels and rabbits and would come down to Brushton to fish on the weekends. It was a hard life for the Stone family, whose only possession was their milk cow, Old Bessy."

"What happened next?" I anxiously coaxed the continuation of a story I'd hear a hundred times.

"First, Old Bessy stopped giving milk, and Mrs. Stone blamed it on the train whistle disturbing the milk cow. Cows can be sensitive that way. Next thing, Old Bessy was dead in her stall, and Mrs. Stone didn't know what to do."

"What happened next?"

"Mrs. Stone got her boys together, and they pulled Old Bessy to the middle of the rail tracks and propped her up to look like she was grazing in the middle of the track."

"But grass don't grow in the middle of the track!" I informed the storyteller.

"That's true! No matter how many blast the train engineer gave, Old Bessy didn't move a muscle."

"Wasn't the cow already dead?" I inquired.

"Old Bessy was sure a goner when the engine's cow catcher bumped Old Bessy down the right-of-way embankment. Mrs. Stone was waiting and ran out screaming at the engineer, 'You've done went and killed my milk cow!' Then she continued, shaking her fist at the passing train while yelling, 'My children not going to have milk to drink!'

"Did the kids have to drink powdered milk?"

"That night they didn't miss the milk because they had steak to eat. Later, the railroad paid for Old Bessy, and Mrs. Stone bought a new milk cow."

"What did she name the new cow?" I asked.

Pa Paw laughed and replied, "She named their new cow C&O."

"Pa Paw, no one names their cow after the railroad!"

"Mrs. Stone did!"

The car eased up the inclined road crossing the track that led to Ridgeview. The sidewalk fronted the old company store and theater building, where several groups of men were gathered. The crowd failed to resemble carefree past Saturday gatherings of shoppers and people waiting for the afternoon movie or a haircut at Pop Lanham's but was instead quiet, as if at a funeral. The sound of a working train could be heard from up the valley where once the humming sound of the mine tipple's unique sounds were the heartbeat of Nellis but were now absent. All that remained was the heavy sulphur smell generated from fires deep in the mountain of slate that filled a valley to the left of the mine tipple. In the past, residents accepted the assaulting perfumed air as a consequence of full employment, but now the stench failed to be a justified recompense to the dying mining town. The mountain of waste was the result of over thirty years of mining activates, where the overburden was separated from the coal shipped to ARMCO steel mills in Ohio and Kentucky. The massive slagheap read like the company ledger's notation, as just a small percentage of the thousands of filled railcars of coal shipped from the now-sealed Nellis mines. At times, fumes from the concealed slate dump fires at Nellis and at Ridgeview would fill the valley with smog so potent it could be tasted with every breath. One Sunday morning, Mom and I were driving to the hillside Nellis Pilgrim Holiness Church, and the smog was so heavy we passed the turnoff to the church.

Every miner's family had a collection of fossils either found at the mine face or retreaded from slate found at the dump, then cracked open to reveal a perfect imprint of an ancient plant leaf. Doors of hillside homes, as well as company houses, were propped open with ancient gray fossils of tree roots and limbs. Mom's father, James (Big Jim) Midkiff, worked at the Red Parrot Mine at Prenter, West Virginia. He had several stalactites retrieved from the mine face when the cutting machine had opened into a concealed pocket of crystals.

The Nellis mine entrance was quickly sealed with a wall of concrete soon after usable mining equipment had been removed. The system of water pumps that pulled water away from the mine face of the steep inclined coal seam were turned off and removed, allowing miles of shafts and rooms to be filled with water. Massive fans that circulated fresh air to the mine face, like the water pumps, were turn off and removed, allowing air to become stale and then replaced by red mine water and black damp.

"Pa Paw, where is Mr. Lanham?" I asked, fearful I was going to get a haircut.

"Pop is enjoying his retirement on his front porch in Brushton." Pa Paw replied as we joined a group closest to the track. The gathering watched while the engine pulled towards the town center. The track was only secondary to the outcropping coal seam that determined the track's end and the location of the mine tipple. The Y arraignment of the track allowed steam engines to change their direction, since their design prevented long runs of a reversed steam engine. The diesel's horn sounded a warning to pedestrians and car drivers of the approaching train as it crossed the Nellis Road for the last time. The train consisted of three loaded coal cars of the last processed load of the tipple. Behind the coal cars, three flat cars loaded with the salvaged mine equipment was destined to ARMCO's new mine at Montcoal, upriver from Brushton above Whitesville.

The gathering stood silent; one man removed his hat and looked to the ground. The horn sounded again, signaling a farewell to Nellis. On the short trip to the junction of the mainline of the C&O Railroad at Brushton, the horn sounded at each crossing, signifying the last passing. Soon people and milk cows walked and cars crossed the track, disregarding the caution exercised for nearly four decades. Train engines would occasionally side track on the spur at Brushton, and the engineer would be seen eating his lunch in the cab of the diesel engine. Later, a coal loading facility would be built at Brushton, and coal cars would be backed up behind the loading tipple and parked. Coal hauled from small truck mines would have coal trucked to the loader, and coal cars dependent upon gravity would be individually released to center under the coal chute. The four cars loaded weekly were but a tease as to Nellis and Ridgeview at their peak.

Chapter 3
A Wake on Joe's Creek

"Mommy, you don't mind watching Johnny?" Lucille Jordan asked her mother.

"Now, Lucille, it's no problem. James and I look forward to spending time with our first grandson," Grandma Midkiff replied, hoping to ease her first child's concern of leaving me for the first time. "Lucille, don't worry. I've raised three families in my life and never had a problem."

"I know, but Johnny can be a handful at times! Mrs. Jordan (Mom always called her mother-in-law, Oma Hudson Jordan, by misses and her-father-in-law, Ted Jordan, as Mr. Jordan) is going to care for Larry but since her mother has been sick, she can't care for both boys and Mrs. Hudson."

"Grandma, can I have a glass of iced tea?" I asked spying the gallon glass jar on the porcelain top of the pie safe. The water at Grandma Midkiff was red with iron and nearly impossible for me to drink, being used to soft water from the community well at Brushton. The Brushton well was drilled when Grandpa Hudson and his brother, Alonzo, built the town of Brushton after they relocated from Peytona as a result of the great flood on Big Coal River in August 1916. Water was provided for the houses they built, housing a population that would support the brick two-story store located trackside in the center of town. Someone else in Bloomingrose must have been repulsed by the hard water that stained clothing, plates, and glasses after continual use, resulted in the tea being so sweet with sugar it was nearly like drinking syrup. In the thick liquid, the sugar magnified anything on the opposite side of the gallon jar.

"Johnny, just a small glass, you know how sugar makes you overactive."

"Sister," Grandpa Midkiff said, "A little sweet tea won't hurt the boy. Now, give him a big glass."

"Daddy, you and Mr. and Mrs. Jordan are spoiling Johnny rotten," Mom replied as she filled a large glass with sweet tea. Grandpa Midkiff was a large man at six feet four inches earning him the nickname of 'Big Jim.' (Years later at the Racine store where I worked, old miners would come in and ask, "You're Big Jim's grandson?")

Mom left after being assured I would be happy at Bloomingrose. Soon, I fell into the cycle that was different than at Brushton. I helped gather eggs from Aunt Lydia's chicken house. Late afternoon, when the sun was starting to shadow behind the mountain peak, we worked in the garden. Grandpa spaded a row of potatoes, breaking the green plants, discarding them to the side marking his progress and serving as a marker as to where to resume at the next day's dig.

"Johnny, pick up the potatoes. They'll be in the clods of dirt. Just drop them in the bucket for dinner." The soil at Bloomingrose, like the water, was different than at Brushton, being red clay. Clods of clay were raised and thrust upon the ground to reveal dinner. "Ednie, Johnny's going to be a farmer someday," Grandpa called across the rows of potatoes, where Grandma was picking green beans and corn. Corn was planted in the spring and later bean seeds planted alongside to grow up the corn stocks used as the vine's support. At Brushton, spring planting was announced when Tunsel Barker, our neighbor with a back yard garden, would come from the mountainside with a tied bundle of three-quarter-inch thick straight sticks he used as bean poles. Tunsel's bean patch had several rows of teepee structures of bean poles for his half-runners of his manicured garden growing in sandy soil. At Bloomingrose, corn stalks supported the bean vines in the hard clay that had yielded crops of fruit and vegetables for over seventy years. "Johnny, keep a sharp eye for Indian arrowheads. George and Harold (mom's brothers) used to find them digging potatoes."

"Grandpa, you mean Indians lived in Bloomingrose?" I asked while breaking another clod of compacted clay. Now, I was more alert for arrowheads than new potatoes.

Grandpa leaned against his hoe, allowing time to catch his breath and to pass down some history of Bloomingrose. "Long before our family moved from Virginia, Shawnee Indians used Big Coal River as their hunting grounds. All the arrowheads you find was a missed rabbit, deer, or bear."

"You mean bears lived in Bloomingrose?" I knew bears lived in Brushton, because I had touched a sleeping bear in Grandma Hudson's November apple tree, but I hadn't considered bears at Bloomingrose. The farm still had a number of apple trees planted years ago to sustain the self-sufficient homestead. Similar to Grandma Hudson's hillside apple orchard, apples were preserved as sweetened sliced apples or apple butter. Apples, like potatoes and onions, were placed in cool root cellars that provided fresh fruit and vegetables for the long winter. In season, fresh apples were sold at both family stores, Hudson Brothers and G. W. Midkiff General Merchandise, to a limited market since most families had their own backyard apple tree or access to a neighbor's tree.

"Ednie!" Grandpa called to his wife, "Johnny has enough potatoes. We're going to the barn to milk Old Daisy."

"James, be careful. Old Daisy kicked my milk pail across the stall yesterday when Susan, Alberta (mom's younger sisters) and I went to do the milking. We ran back to the house and Harold and George (mom's younger brothers) had to do the milking." She then closed with "I don't want Lucille to worry!"

The unpainted wood barn was located at the break of the descending mountain away from the homestead, allowing a distance of air to dilute barn smells. To the barn's front, a fenced garden of cucumbers, melons, mustard, green onions, cabbage, leaf lettuce, and sweet potatoes grew. During the 1950s, the farm still functioned, although grape and raspberry vines and apple trees were never replaced after dying. The yearly practice of planting a vegetable garden, buying chicks at Mason's to replace ones served at Sunday dinner, and the purchase of three hogs served to continue the idea of a working farm. Two crabapple trees in Aunt Lydia's yard remained, producing a mass of fallen fruit covered with honey bees and yellow jackets, but like the fallen June apples they no longer were burdened to sustain the homestead.

"Johnny, stand away from Old Daisy. Don't know what's made her ornery! I don't want Sister to worry about you!" he said as he placed a galvanized pail under Old Daisy and pulled up an upturned five-gallon metal bucket that served as his seat.

"Grandpa, was this barn here when you were a boy?" I inquired as I looked at the decrepit barn. It was my first time inside the barn. "This is a big barn for one cow!"

"Poppy built the barn after Aunt Lydia's house," he said while pulling on the cow's teats. "Mules and horses were keep in the barn's back half, and hay filled the loft. Why, when a cloud burst hit the river, we lived in the loft for several weeks and were lucky to have a dry place."

The pail was filled; as we walked, returning to the house, past Aunt Lydia's chicken coop, milk slopped over the top edge. A cat scented the milk and chased behind, stopping to lap milk puddled on the hard ground. The soil provided nourishment for the family from the cows grazing on grass to the apples on the scattered trees.

"James, I scalded the churn. It's ready for you," Grandma said as we entered the rear kitchen door. The kitchen remained the working center of the family farm. Daisy's milk was poured into the slender stoneware churn, and Grandpa took a seat next to the butter churn. He moved the wood dasher with a rhythm timed with conversation. "Johnny, do you want to make butter?" Grandpa asked, seeing I had finished my glass of syrupy iced tea.

"Could I?" Pa Paw said I'm a good worker, and Ma Maw said I needed to do work so I would stay out of trouble." I quickly came to stand by the porcelain churn. "Ma Maw said she had to keep me busy just to keep her place from being destroyed." Taking the wood plunger smooth with years of wear I asked, "What are we making Grandpa?"

"Johnny, you're making butter. All the Midkiffs grew up liking homemade butter. What kind of butter do you eat at home?"

"Mom buys Chiffon at the store."

Grandpa cautioned. "Johnny, slow down. You're splashing the milk, and the butter needs to be made slowly." It was obvious I was growing tired.

That night I slept with Grandma upstairs on the mountain side room that connected to a riverside twin room. Perhaps, it was just life on the farm of early to bed and early to rise, but time passes slowly, I could actually see the illuminated minute hand of the clock move with every tick. One single window centered at each end of the second-story bedrooms were absent of any cooling breeze. In early morning, a welcome rush of cool air descended from the mountainside, offering a reprieve from the smoldering heat. The tin roof announced the temperature change with pops and squeaks as the metal contracted, pulling against nails and rafters.

"Get up, Johnny! It's time to go to church," Grandma Midkiff called from the kitchen.

"I just got to sleep. The noisy roof kept me awake," I pleaded and rolled over.

"Johnny, the tin roof was just singing a song. James can't sleep without the sound of the pops and squeaks," she added.

"Grandma, the old roaster kept me awake all night crowing. Tunsel Barker's chickens didn't keep me awake all night crowing in Brushton!" I countered.

"Johnny, it wouldn't be Bloomingrose without our blind rooster." Then she explained, "The old rooster knows it's his job to crow, but doesn't know when the sun is up. So he crows all night, doing his job, hoping Lydia doesn't invite him for Sunday dinner."

"Grandma, do you think Tunsel invited his roosters to Sunday dinner since they don't crow?" I questioned, as I crawled from the now uncomfortable bed, already getting warm from the heat transferred from the tin roof.

"I'm sure his roosters were invited to Sunday dinner! Come on down now. We need to walk to church."

The Midkiff family was "Church of Christ", as much as Grandpa Hudson was a Methodist, and Ma Maw Oma was a Pilgrim. The white clapboard church building was centered in town between the farm and Aunt Esther and Uncle Marion's home. The roadside morning walk to church squeezed us close to the ditch by passing cars was in response to the morning dew that collected on the grass and weeds. Sunday traffic was limited; but still, rear-approaching traffic encouraged a fast walk. Similar to the noise of a singing tin roof and a blind rooster crowing through the night, the sound of speeding cars traveling during the night, was different than at Brushton. The noise of cars traveling downriver became noticeable out of the curve at Morton's Store, a mile above the farm. The sound, resembled the wind, growing during the car's approach, and then the sound would decrease as the car moved downriver, away from the farm, like a retreating echo. Cars on Brushton's roads lacked the straight-away to produce a sound louder than the sound of red dog from the Nellis slate dump, used on unpaved roads, crushing against the tires. The sound of the train was diluted by the distance across the blacktopped two-lane road and the river, unlike the train's roar as it passed fifty feet from Brushton bedrooms. Bloomingrose residents would have been startled from a sound sleep by passing coal trains.

Regardless of whether a community was planned, like the company town of Nellis, or grew from a single farmhouse into a named town like Brushton or Bloomingrose, a church to serve the community was always among the first public building. Great-grandpa G. W. Midkiff donated land for the Bloomingrose Church of Christ, like at Brushton, where Great-grandpa Hudson gave land for the Methodist Church on the hillside above their home.

The raised church building rested on a raised basement that housed Sunday school classrooms nearly identical to basement classrooms of the Ashford Church of God (Holiness), Brushton Methodist, Ridgeview Presbyterian, and the Nellis Pilgrims. A simple steeple housing a bell rested on the pitched roof above the front double door. The Bloomingrose bell sounded a five-minute warning for late worshippers and announced weddings celebrations and funeral farewells up and down the valley. The church bell once also served as a warning for a rise in the river or a house fire, but now the bell was relegated to church affairs by televisions, telephones, and travel by car that made the alarm bell nearly obsolete. The church bell was recognized by its unique sound like a region's distinctive accent. Once when Grandma Edna was attending a funeral at the Brushton Methodist Church the church bell was sounded to bid farewell, and Grandma commented the church bell sounded just the same as it did fifty years before when it rang for the Peytona Baptist Church.

"Grandma how do you know that?" I asked, wondering how a church bell at Brushton could be heard over five miles up-river at Peytona.

"The church building was washed down the river, and people said the building stayed together for the five-mile trip and the bell rang until the building crashed against the C&O railroad bridge at Brushton."

"What happened then?" I asked as we stood to follow the casket from the church.

She continued, "The church building broke apart, and the heavy bell sunk by the bridge. Mr. Hudson was building this church, and he rescued the bell."

"Did the Baptist bell sound different when it became a Methodist bell?" I asked then added, "Ma Maw told me there's a big difference between being a Methodist and a Pilgrim, but I know their Easter eggs taste the same."

"No different, Johnny. People said it was God's hand that protected the floating building down the

Big Coal River to find a new home in Brushton. Every Sunday it still calls people to come to church."

The Nellis Presbyterian Church, situated on the hillside beside the elementary school, was the only exception to the community's style of church buildings, being a plastered building sporting stained glass windows, a massive steeple, and central heat. The plastered building was painted in a two-tone style with off white and a pale light green that blended with the company town of Nellis. ARMCO built the school building and church building to provide needed facilities for their workers.

Inside the church building, Grandma Edna, Alberta, and Susan took their seats where they had since the first service in 1936. Even when a member was not at Sunday service, respect was shown for a family's pew claim, and the preacher knew of someone's absence with a glance from the raised chancel. Aunt Lydia, along with her sisters, Esther and Louise, and their husbands sat together. Later, they would have Sunday dinner at Aunt Esther's home. Grandma Midkiff's mother, Great-grandma Virgie Mae Barker and Grandma Edna's sister, Hazel, sat near the front in order to hear the choir. Later they would have Sunday dinner at their home, across the small creek from Aunt Lydia's house, followed by front porch visiting and time in their front yard vegetable garden. In the Church of Christ tradition, the interior's unadorned white walls and ceiling blended with the windows that lined both walls, providing light and a breeze when opened during the summer, but nothing more.

After Sunday school in the basement, church

service started. The sanctuary, now half-filled, waited for the adult church service. Mr. Cantley signaled the start of service by sounding a pitch tuner, and the choir replied until they were in unison. The choir sang acapella since musical instruments aren't mentioned in the New Testament, and the sound of the Bloomingrose choir was different than Brother Lakin's group of Pilgrim singers accompanied with a piano, being pure human voice that rose and fell in tempo more akin to a voice from mountain people. (Now, I understand their love of pure human voice in singing praise.)

Members congregated at the front of the church while the church bell announced the close of service, and most walked home. Some crossed the two-lane road to the Bloomingrose swing bridge. Many communities utilized suspension bridges to access across-the-river family homes and small settlements once only accessible by a shallow river crossing near rocky river shoals. The bridge's design was universally shared with other Big Coal River crossings, having twin towers on each side of ten-inch pipe. A matching one-and-a-half-inch cable crossed the river, supporting the wood pathway. The cable was locked in a concrete dead man that made for a convenient seat for people waiting for a ride or loafers. The towers of the Bloomingrose Bridge were distinctive, being painted pink. I reasoned the pink towers somehow were related to the name of the community, Bloomingrose, since roses are pink, but the unique pink was a result of years of weather greeting a coating of red-lead paint.

I was always fascinated by the suspension

bridges, but was fearful since riding my Uncle Pete, Dad's brother, piggy-back from the deck of the bridge into the swimming hole at the Wirehouse above Brushton. The rite-of-passage, jumping from the bridge, is now unavailable to swimmers, but to me remains a fear of heights, like the concrete dead heads and cut steel cables resting on the ground at the Wirehouse.

"Johnny, stay close, the horseweeds are high in Poppy's Field and some are still wet," Grandma Midkiff warned as we walked home. "Can't have your Sunday clothes spoiled, we need to go to Mrs. Sutton's wake tonight." Poppy's Field was a flat field overgrown with weeds between the "Farm" and the Church of Christ. A footpath wormed its way through the jungle. Grandma Barker and Hazel avoided the dangerous narrow roadside path when walking to church risking wet shoes and clothes from the morning dew.

"James, we're home," Grandma Midkiff called to her husband. Although Grandpa had been churched in the Church of Christ, he claimed he had been over-churched and had spent ample time as a child sitting on a hard cold church pew. With the exception of funerals, he never walked through Poppy's Field with us to church, nor did he partake in Sunday dinner at Aunt Esther's, but stayed at home to prepare Sunday dinner.

"Ednie, dinner will be ready soon. The pork roast needs to cook just a little longer to be right," he said as he sat in one of the padded kitchen chairs. "Pour Johnny a big glass of ice tea. I know he is dry after a morning of churching!"

"Grandpa, why do you sit in the chair backwards?" I asked, wondering about the unusually sitting position.

"Why Johnny, most people get only half the use a chair can give. I sit backwards, and all I need to do is step backwards and I'm standing and able to attend our pork roast cooking on the stove." I was satisfied with his reasoning and recalled Ma Maw Oma telling about the first time she met Mr. Midkiff, and he was seated backwards in a kitchen chair.

"Mr. Midkiff! John Edward and Lucille are just too young to be married!" Ma Maw insisted. Ma Maw had Pa Paw drive her to Bloomingrose to protest Dad and Mom's marriage when they eloped to Catlettsburg, Kentucky.

Grandpa Midkiff listened to his daughter's new mother-in-law and calmly replied, "Mrs. Jordan, they are young and the best we can do is support them and help them when we can." Later Ma Maw (laughing) told me of her first meeting and always mentioned that Mr. Midkiff was sitting backwards in a kitchen chair.

"Ma Maw Jordan always has fired chicken for Sunday dinner," I commented. "Is it alright to eat pork on Sunday? Pa Paw always had fried pork chops on Saturday night."

"Johnny, we won't tell Mrs. Jordan you had pork roast for Sunday dinner?" It was a simple solution, obvious to everyone, knowing when dealing with Ma Maw it was easier to ask for forgiveness rather than for permission, not that it mattered.

"Johnny, we're going over to visit with Grandma Barker," Grandma Midkiff told me. We walked back towards the church and stopped at the raised house situated on a rounded extension of the hillside. I always thought of the hillside as an ideal Indian burial mound, but the hard packed clay prevented exploration for arrowheads. "Johnny, Grandma has carrot cake. Do you want a slice?" Someone inquired in hopes of keeping me busy, pre-warned by Mom of my habit of getting into trouble. "It's Grandma Barker's favorite."

"Sure would!" I responded, thinking it would be as sweet as syrupy iced tea. Ma Maw Oma was known for her pie baking with homemade crust for apple, lemon, and chocolate marinade pies. On holidays, she varied by baking pumpkin and pecan pies and cakes for birthdays, but never carrot cake. Carrot cake was never a favorite for me, and it was the only cake ever available at Grandma Barker's, encourage by a patch of carrots in her garden.

Aunt Hazel's daughter, Shirley Snodgrass, accompanied by her husband, Charles, their son, Greg, that was my age, and their daughter, Capitola, would often come to visit Grandma Barker, and it offered a diversion from typical church, farm, and weather talk. The house was without indoor plumbing, and water had to be carried from the well in the back yard. The eight-inch pipe rose from the hard packed ground, and a pulley centered above the pipe where a six-inch diameter galvanized pipe (that resembled a stove pipe) was attached that could be lowered into the well head and would descend to the water level where it would sink. The attachment would be raised, and the weight of the water would cause the trap at the bottom to close and a tube of water could be lifted. It was a surprise that water was still in the well, since Larry and I always carried a pocket of gravel to drop into the water well to hear the splash. Unlike the red hard water at the farm, Grandma Barker's water was soft and sweet like the water at Brushton.

"Johnny, you stayed clean today! It would be a shame to go to tonight's service with your clothes spoiled!" Grandma Midkiff said, relieved that I still was presentable. "Now, we're going to ride up to Joe's Creek with Lydia to wake Mrs. Sutton. Remember to be quiet and keep all your questions for our ride home," Grandma instructed.

The Midkiff family, besides being a "Church of Christ" family, was also a "Ford" family as strong as Ma Maw Oma was a "Pilgrim" and Pa Paw was a "Chevrolet" man. Aunt Lydia always owned a black four-door Ford, perhaps a carryover from Henry Ford's black Model T, as habits changed slowly at Bloomingrose.

"Johnny, mind what you say at the wake. Don't ask any questions about Mrs. Sutton's old house! Do you understand?" Aunt Lydia had been the Midkiff family's matriarch since her father died in 1936, and many family members would argue she ran the show soon after her birth in 1899. She was a seasoned principal at Seth Elementary and had dealt with stubborn students most of her life. "Johnny, do you think I'm going to die soon?" She questioned me when I casually mentioned I wanted her old farmhouse when she died. "Johnny, you take the cake," was her final response.

Another time, I was with her in what she called

the "canning room," a small room off her kitchen equipped with a stove, working tables, and a single-bowl porcelain sink. It all started when Pa Paw gave money to Aunt Francis Hudson for real cowboy boots all the way from Oklahoma where she was going to visit her sister, Ruth. Larry liked his boots so much he slept in them. I proudly wore mine everywhere.

"Ted, Johnny can't wear his cowboy boots to church! He makes so much noise," Ma Maw Oma informed her husband before we were leaving for church. "Johnny you need to wear regular shoes like Pa Paw to church. What would people think, wearing such flashy shoes!"

"Ma Maw, Aunt Francis said everyone in Oklahoma wears cowboy boots like kids here wear PF Flyers," I argued. "Cowboys wear their boots to church in Oklahoma!" I countered and hoped I could slip into the back seat of the car and not be discovered until it was too late when we were at church.

"Ted, I swear he walks just to hear his boots click against the floor. He even wanted me to take up the living room rug! I scolded him about the noise. Ted, he told me the boots were just talking. That sounded a lot like something he heard you say!"

"Now, Oma. You are always asking where the boy is, and what's he up to. His noisy boots should put you at easy since you'll always know where he is, and if you don't hear boot clicks, then you know to check up on him. He's just a boy!"

"Ted, it would ease my worry always knowing where the boy is," She reasoned.

"Aunt Lydia, you see my sharp-toed cowboy boots? I'm going to kick your eyes out if you don't stop burning your trash in Grandma Midkiff's back yard!" Aunt Lydia was in the habit of using a burn pile directly by Grandma's house, preventing the smell of smoke in her yard.

"Johnny, that doesn't sound like you. I know where you heard such mean talk!" She was stunned but remained composed as we walked next door to Grandma Midkiff's house by the enclosed hallway that connected the houses. "George, little Johnny just told me he was going to kick my eyes out with his sharp-toed cowboy boots if I didn't stop burning trash in the yard, and I know he couldn't have thought of such mean words by himself! He's just repeating what he has heard."

"Lydia, I didn't say any such thing!" George said in defense.

"Come along Johnny. I have some hard candy in my purse." We returned to Aunt Lydia's house, and I enjoyed several pieces of hard candy. George had made the mistake of quarreling in front of me about Aunt Lydia burning trash in their yard. The reference to my pointed boots was my invention, but Aunt Lydia recognized her mistake and started burning trash out by her driveway.

Joe's Creek was a wide valley above Bloomingrose, famous for an oilfield discovery by the Pure Oil Company with over a hundred oil wells scattered in people's backyards. People tolerated the constant whine of pumping jacks, the hum of the gathering station, the pungent odor of oil and natural gas, and the big load trucks that congested the narrow road. Unless employed by Pure Oil or an oil contractor, people received no compensation in the form of royalties since the mineral rights were owned by corporations.

"Johnny! Mind your manners," Aunt Lydia gave instructions before I bounded from the back seat of the black Ford. "Ednie, we'll have to keep a close hold on the boy. You know how he gets when his curiosity is raised."

"Lydia, we may need to cut our visit short!" said Grandma Midkiff. The Sutton place hugged the hillside like many early mountain home that saved the flat bottomland for farming. Settlers cleared sections of hillside to accommodate grazing needs, but the thin mountainside soil limited productivity. The weathered house was unpainted with a long porch that span the front that provided a covered area for a farm's table work and a place to visit on a Sunday afternoon. A group of old men gathered on the porch, and the smell of Prince Albert tobacco scented the air. The loose package tobacco of Prince Albert (in a tin) or Bugler (in a cellophane wrapped paper container) were common tobacco products for people that always used loose tobacco or a dirt poor replacement for manufactured store-bought cigarettes. Grandpa Hudson's bedroom always smelled of Prince Albert pipe tobacco, and the Methodist were tolerant of tobacco use. Uncle Alonzo (Aunt Louise's husband) an avid "Church of Christ" member, enjoyed cheroots cigars, and since the church was so set against musical instrument accompaniment, the use of the "Devil's cabbage" would not have been unreasonable considering there was no mention of tobacco use in the New Testament. Church of Christ members, the Methodist, and Pilgrims abstained from drinking wine; although numerous citations of Jesus using wine are in the New Testament, it never mentions Jesus relaxed with his Disciples and having a smoke. The prohibited use of spirited drinks, the use of the Lord's Prayer, and the avoidance of foul language were the only universally accepted practices of the Baptist, Methodist, and Pilgrims.

"Miss Midkiff," (Aunt Lydia was always addressed as Miss being an old maid) Clarence Smith, an old family friend, called to her as we stepped onto the rickety porch. "Ednie, who do you have with you? He looks a lot like Big Jim (my Grandpa Midkiff's nickname)."

"Clarence, this is Lucille's son, Johnny. He has a lot of Midkiff in him."

"But I don't like homemade butter. Grandpa said all the Midkiffs like Daisy's butter. I like Chiffon from the store. Mom said I'm big boned like the Midkiffs," I continued to talk.

"Ednie, Johnny's on a talking roll. We'll need to keep him close at hand," Aunt Lydia sighed.

"Lydia, I know!" Grandma remarked, "Johnny this is like church. We don't do a lot of talking."

"Pa Paw always gives me Juicy Fruit gum to keep me quiet."

"Lydia, do you have any Juicy Fruit?"

"No, Ednie, but I do have a purse full of hard candy." Then she added, "Take a hand full and keep it close by in your pocket. At the first sign of trouble, give Johnny a piece of hard candy."

We passed into the house, stepping down from the porch level to a hard packed dirt floor. Throw rugs were scattered around the long room and mourners stood in small groups or were seated at table chairs borrowed from the kitchen. "Grandma, where's the floor?" I inquired since the only building I ever visited without a floor was Daisy's barn.

"Ednie, hurry! Give Johnny a piece of hard candy!" Aunt Lydia encouraged hoping, to quiet my inquiry.

Grandma handed me a piece of candy as she bent over to whisper in my ear, "Johnny, save your questions for the ride home!" She then glanced at Aunt Lydia saying, "Lydia, it's either going to be a long evening or a very short one!" Aunt Lydia indicated agreement with a positive nod of her head.

The house was a typical homestead with the front room serving as a formal gathering place and the adjoining kitchen as the working heart of the family farm. At the end of the front room, the body of Mrs. Sutton laid in state with hanging kerosene lanterns illuminating the room. She rested on a quilt-covered table as if sleeping. Another quilt covered the bottom portion of her body replicating the closed bottom half of a casket door. It was customary for new arrivals to approach the reposed body in a show of respect. Grandma held one on my hands and Aunt Lydia the other as we approached. "Johnny, we need to show respect for Mrs. Sutton so don't talk, Aunt Lydia, trained in school discipline, instructed.

"Aunt Lydia, she just looks like she's asleep up on the kitchen table," I commented.

"Ednie give him another piece of hard candy," Aunt Lydia suggested. "How long do you think we need to stay to show respect?"

"Lydia, we have maybe enough hard candy for an hour."

"Ednie, give me a warning when you give Johnny the last piece, and we will leave before he makes Mrs. Sutton's wake the talk of Joe's Creek!"

"I just hope we have enough for an hour of silence. I know why Mr. Jordan always has a pocket of Juicy Fruit. Mrs. Jordan would sure be passing a gallstone, Johnny's always talking about, if she were here tonight," Aunt Lydia added. "I may pass a big one before the evenings over, Ednie."

"Why, Lydia, you've never had gallstones before!" Grandma Midkiff added.

"Ednie, I've never taken Johnny to a wake before either!"

On the way to Bloomingrose, I rode in the front seat between the two women. I didn't need an invitation to ask questions. "Grandma, why did Mrs. Sutton's house have a dirt floor?"

"Johnny, Mrs. Sutton raised her family in that house. The front room was used for wakes for the whole Sutton family. It was Mrs. Sutton's last request to have her wake at her old home."

"How did she live in a house with dirt floors?" I was fascinated by the floors. Dad told me when he was a boy, the front yards at all the houses in Brushton were hard packed ground, and a blade of grass didn't grow, because people used their front yards in the evening to sit. It was their summertime front room.

"Her son, Earl, removed the old rotten floor and tamped the soil to make it hard packed. When the family lived at the place it had regular floors."

Aunt Lydia concluded, hoping my question had been answered.

"Johnny you can tell Grandpa all about the wake when we get back to Bloomingrose." Grandma Midkiff added, hoping to pass on the question and answer game to a fresh source.

"Okie-dokie! Can I have a glass of your sweet tea when we get back?" I asked. "I've had enough hard candy!"

Chapter 4
Last Steam Train Through Brushton

"Johnny, I can't see anything!" My younger brother, Larry, yelled over the roar of the steam engine as it passing through Brushton. Larry and I hid behind Ma Maw's front porch glider while the steam engine passed. Steam engines were the work horses pulling up and down Big Coal River for the last forty years, and would have been replaced by the more efficient diesel engines earlier, if not for the economic turndown of the Great Depression and the need for all new equipment diverted to the war effort during the Second World War. Steam engines continued to pull coal into the mid-century due to an increased demand for coal, and new diesel engines were unavailable to replace antiquated steam as the C&O Railroad would have wanted.

Economic was the driving force that killed the use of steam on the railroads. The workhorses of American railroads were doomed to the scrap yards, since ledge book comparisons ran red when steam was compared to diesel. Just the supporting facilities needed for steam were duplicated on every mainline, and branch line included water, coal, and sand towers; water pumping stations; turn-tables; and large maintenance and repair shops. Labor was another negative aspect of steam, requiring a two-man team, an engineer and a fireman, on every engine, along with an army of highly skilled craftsmen to maintain the constant need to service and replace worn moving parts. The tremendous weight of the engine required expensive bridges capable of carrying the weight, and the track life was challenged by the extra load and a loaded tender car of fuel coal and water. Diesel's had the advantage of have the ability to run mainline in either direction just by the swivel on the engineer's seat, where steam engines need a turntable or a Y layout to accomplish a reverse run.

Steam declines, as did passenger service, during the 1950s, resulting in streamlined diesel passenger engines reduced to pull coal and freight trains. Seeing a degraded two-unit passenger engine pulling coal up Big Coal River was as out-of-place as a well-dressed lady taking a hobo to a dance.

"Johnny, take my hand! The "doodlebug" is coming. I hear its horn at the Morrison crossing." The "doodlebug" was equipped with a gasoline engine that turned a generator, powering a traction motor attached to the car's axle. The single car transported passengers up Big Coal River, at one time, it delivered the US mail and freight before truck delivery became commonplace. Like steam power, the "doodlebug" was an antiquated remnant of the past. Local believed the given name "doodlebug" was a local-only moniker, but since the self-powered unit's development, it was known as a "doodlebug" throughout the national rail system.

"Johnny, don't scuff your new shoes!" Ma Maw instructed me while I was kicking at the compacted cinders retrieved from fireboxes of steam engines. The railroad platform that fronted my grandparent's home, like the steam engine, was obsolete since passengers soon wouldn't wait for the "doodlebug," and train freight was no longer delivered at Brushton. At one time, a small fright office was located at the upriver end, along with a place for a one-man handcar used for track inspection and light maintenance. Another rail side platform abutted the dead-end Brush Creek rail line indicating once people waited for the "doodlebug" to Nellis but was obscured by encroaching weeds and brush due to disuse.

"Johnny, hand him our money," came instructions as we stepped up into the car. The car was like a bus on the rail, with seat on both sides and operating controls on both ends that allowed to car to make a return trip without have to turn the car. "Johnny sit by the window," Ma Maw suggested in hopes I would make a memory of the trip. She recalled taking the "doodlebug" to St. Albans, at the mouth of Big Coal River and the Kanawha River and catching a public bus to Charleston to shop, and making a return trip to Brushton on the evening run.

"Ma Maw, you sure must have liked shopping in Charleston to take the "doodlebug." Why didn't you ride with Pa Paw?" I asked while looking through the window.

"Ted was drafted and in Belgium during the war; beside, gasoline was rationed, and I couldn't drive." Dad enjoyed telling about Ma Maw being so embarrassed when waited at the Brushton station for his proud mother coming home from a Saturday shopping trip. It was before she became a Pilgrim, abandoning worldly apparel. Dad waited in a 1928 Essex sedan that once belonged to his Grandfather

George Jordan. The car was rough, and Ma Maw wearing a stole, was red-in-the-face with embarrassment, refusing a ride, walking home.

After Brushton, few houses were upriver until Peytona, where we stopped. At the duplicate rail side platform, one of Ma Maw nephews waited to give us a ride across the river to Aunt Cora's, Ma Maw's older sister, home. It would have been a short walk across the river if we could have used the abandon bridge that crossed into lower Peytona. The wood deck of the bridge had been removed, and a barrier braced against the girders of the truss bridge. The rusty relic was of special pride for Aunt Lydia, since her father's name, G.W. Midkiff, a county commissioner, was embossed on an iron plate attached to the center cross member under 1912. A bridge at Seth and one at Danville crossing the Little Coal River were duplicate bridges and held equal places of pride for Aunt Lydia. When Aunt Lydia's brother said he hoped he died before Lydia because it would kill everyone trying to dig a grave big enough to bury all of Poppy's things with Lydia when she died, I'm sure he included the three bridges.

Peytona proper was little changed since Grandpa Hudson moved his family to Brushton after the flood of 1916. The old Hudson house remained alongside the store building, now used as a meeting place for the Knights of Pythias (KPs). Grandpa Hudson was a proud member along with his son, Reginald (Giggs), and my Dad. Ma Maw Oma didn't condemn the Lodge nor supported it. Before the flood, the riverside town was connected by wagon roads across Short Creek Mountain and by a canal system build to haul Cannel Coal from mines above Peytona and on Drawdy Creek. The new railroad made the canal obsolete and the flood washed away the eight locks that pooled water, enabling barge navigation.

"Johnny, it nice you and Oma came to visit," Aunt Cora greeted us at the door. Cora had red hair like Grandpa Hudson along with their brother, Hubert, (Uncle Red). She was a favorite relative, and I recalled an earlier visit when she served desert.

"Aunt Cora, did you make your special cake and ice cream?" I eagerly inquired, recalling our last visit.

"I made it yesterday evening and put it in the freezer so it would be just right." Her special cake was created from broken pieces of an angel food cake mixed with soft vanilla ice cream and refrozen in a molded bowl.

We sat in the living room, and I had a second serving of desert while the sisters visited and talked about family. They were of different makeup, Cora being a Presbyterian, Eastern Star member, and a Republican. Ma Maw never talked politics, leaving that to Pa Paw and Dad, so they held their visit to family and the weather.

"Oma, you and Johnny come again for a visit. I'll always have dessert, Johnny," Cora said as we were leaving. Unlike other homes, the Bradley family had enclosed the once-open front porch into a sunroom. I asked Ma Maw why it was a sunroom if it was always dark. I was fascinated by a large pressure gauge suspended on a three-eighth-inch pipe used to indicate line pressure for the Indian Creek Gas

Company that was owned by the Bradley family.

"Aunt Cora, if we come, it won't be on the 'doodlebug.'"

"That's right. The 'doodlebug' is making its last trip."

American industry was changing at a rapid pace, and the change could be marked in the coal field sometime in drastic examples and often in un-noticed ways. Large blocks of lump coal made up the majority of coal cars for forty years, but gradually changed to smaller pieces of coal, and finally to powder. One or two cars loaded with large lump coal would be at the end of the train next to the red wood caboose (#90997), and, like lump coal, would be soon replaced by a blinking end-of-train device (ETD).

The extensive support system needed by steam engines remained alone the trackside of the C&O line. People liked the reminder of a past steam era, romanticizing black choking smoke, the air filled with ash and cinders, the noise, and the smell of grease and steam exhaust. Steam enthusiasts were encouraged relics that remained in place, hoping for a return of steam, but eventually, without fanfare, a work train and crew worked their way upriver and completed to process of erasing steam from the roadbed's right-of-way.

Across the river from Brushton, fronting the Libbey-Owens-Ford gas compressor station, the C&O Railroad maintained a water station that included a trackside standing water tank, located across the tracks, where a raised control building for the *w*ater facility stood, closer to the river a massive water storage tank, and a riverside building housing engines and pumps to lift river water to the first storage tank where gravity was utilizes to fill back ends of tender cars.

The work crew did quick work removing the water tower and chute, un-ceremonially loading it along with the cut up massive water tank on an open flat car destine to the scrape yard. The control office was pulled down and scooped into a low side gondola car, along with the pulled down pumping station. When the work train pulled up river, all that remained was footprints of the past steam era, the railroad's telephone booth, and the Brushton sign suspended on an 8 by 8 post that resembled a crucifix minus its headrest post.

Automation in the coal mines resulted in a decline in needed workers similar to the labor-intense steam decline in workers. Track maintenance was labor-intense, with large numbers of men needed for section crews during major repair or replacement. Even day-to-day operations required manpower to travel a section of rail on a handcar, looking for damaged rail, missing or loose spikes, or rock slides. The track above Brushton, referred to as the "Narrows," hugged the mountainside, following the curve of the hillside resulting in an area of curves in the track. There was a noted difference in the sound of the straining diesel working against the added track friction due to the curved track. Track wear was excessive in the area, and inspection and replacement was a consent. The C&O determined it was more economic to install an automatic greasing system to decrease the rail's wear. This resulted in the engine's traction wheels often spinning on the slick track, but the corporation determined it could save money using more fuel rather than replacing rails.

Daily, the section worker, Tye Barker, would leave from Ashford and travel on his one-man handcart upriver to inspect the track. "Hi Uncle Tye!" I called as he passed Brushton. His eyes were constantly surveying the track, searching for cracked rails or other problems. He would pull his handcart off the mainline whenever a coal train was scheduled to pass.

A large number of current and retired railroad workers live along the river. Tye Barker's family were mostly railroad people. His older brother, Uncle Vess, was a section worker retired to his place in Brushton. He and his wife, Odie, spent their days on their front porch waving to passers-by. I was always fascinated by the old couple, his wife, like Mrs. Hale, continued to wear a 19th century sun bonnet while always smoking Three Brothers tobacco in a corncob pipe. His brother, Uncle Daley, lived up Brush Creek with his wife, Auntie, and spent his retirement after working forty years for the C&O bird and rabbit hunting. Dad sometimes went deer hunting with Uncle Daley making trips to Pocahontas County. Dad claimed a deer would have to pack its lunch to cross Boone County, since so much of the forest had been clear-cut and was still recovering. Game and fish that once abounded in Boone County forests and streams supported early pioneers, but when their habitat was destroyed, their numbers were decimated.

Chapter 5
Bloomingrose Family Stories

"Johnny, it's time to go to sleep. I'm sure Mrs. Jordan has you to bed early," Aunt Lydia said to encourage me to slow down. It had been a busy day at Bloomingrose, and she was usually a late night person but somewhat exhausted chasing after me. At the chicken house she had told me, "Johnny we don't need to gather the eggs again." And I responded, "Can I give them some more cracked corn?" Sleeping at Aunt Lydia's was much more comfortable than in Grandma Midkiff' hot upstairs bedroom. The old farmhouse was even more sound proof against a blind roaster in the habit of crowing throughout the night.

I liked the old farmhouse that her Poppy has built 60 years before with virgin poplar milled at the Lackawanna Lumber Company at Seth. The two-story house was no longer practical, being so large for just Aunt Lydia to live in, but when build it provided rooms for Great- great-grandpa James Midkiff and his wife, Martha James Midkiff. Three brothers and three sisters were raised in the house, and Aunt Lydia said when she was a girl, room were often let to traveling salesmen. But the house always held my attention and always raised a debate, in my mind, while counting rooms: should an upstairs' hallway with a bed be counted as a room, or should the sunporch, well room, canning room, or hallway, that connected Grandpa Midkiff house with Aunt Lydia's, be counted as rooms. Regardless, the house was larger than houses in Brushton.

Upstairs the bedrooms were as if deceased family members had left and were expected to return. Uncle Joel's suits hung in his cedar robe and Uncle Raymond's open package of cigarettes remained on his dresser. A memorial of family members with death dates hung in the bedroom hallway, whose frame was missing some plaster work as a result of flood damage sustained in the great flood of 1916. A photo of Martha James Midkiff hung in her bedroom with a painted portrait of her husband displayed on the opposite wall. The front down rivers bedroom was Aunt Lydia's mother, Alberta Sutphin Midkiff's, ("Other Mom"), room, which was extra fancy with a finished oak floor. The upstairs walls were four-inch beaded board milled of virgin yellow popular.

"Pa Paw always tells me a story and I go right to sleep!" I countered. Aunt Lydia was known as a late night person, and so was I.

"I see what Lucille was talking about!" Aunt Lydia said under her breath. "One story, and you go to sleep."

"I promise!" I propped up to hear the story because Aunt Lydia was a skilled story teller.

"Upstairs in the upriver bedroom a picture of your Great-great-grandmother Midkiff is on the wall. Before she was married her last name was James. She was the sister to Jesse James' father." She hesitated waiting for my reaction which didn't occur. "Do you know anything about Jesse James?" She followed up, "People said he was like Robin Hood, robbing trains and banks and giving the money to poor people that need it."

"Ma Maw Oma said taking what's not yours is a

sin!" I replied defending my upbringing.

"Johnny, let me finish the story so you can go to sleep," she insisted.

"When the law was chasing him, he would come to Bloomingrose to stay with his Aunt Martha."

"Aunt Lydia no one knew him. Wasn't his picture on TV?"

"No Johnny. TV wasn't invented yet. This was over seventy- years ago."

"What did people do without TV? I asked.

"Johnny everyone worked so hard on the farm they just wanted to go to sleep. If they had TVs, they would have turned them off and gone to sleep. Just like you need to do!"

"What happened next?"

"Jesse needed to hide out and he also need a job."

"Aunt Lydia, you said he robbed trains. Wouldn't he have plenty money. What would he get on a coal train?"

She had expected an easy time telling a bedtime story, but it was proving difficult. "Out west gold and silver were carried on trains." Then added, "he gave all the gold away and needed a job."

"Like loads of coal?" I asked.

"No. The gold was in a safe in the mail car."

"Anyway, he and his brother Frank opened a shoe store in Seth." She went on, "people at Seth needed shoes."

"You mean people didn't get their shoes at Sears. Pa Paw takes me to Sears when I need new shoes."

Aunt Lydia lacked expressions used by Ma Maw Oma like "Lord give me strength," being a seasoned teacher. She found that a lack of expression offered an advantage on not showing one needs help or is at a loss. So she offered a moment of silence hoping I would just listen to her tale and not made more inquiries.

"One day they closed their store after selling out of shoes and went back out West to rob more trains so they could give money to the poor."

"Did they give any of their shoe money to the poor? Ma Maw Oma said a little part of Pa Paw's pay goes to the church to do work for Jesus." I was intrigued that a relative robbed banks.

She had wished she had told a different tall tale but couldn't make a quick end of the tale. "Grandpa James was sitting on the front porch and a stranger came up to the porch."

"Who was the stranger?"

"Johnny, I'm getting to that. Give me time!" Then asked hopefully, "aren't you getting sleepy? We need to gather eggs and feed the chickens tomorrow."

"The stranger was a detective working for the last railroad Jesse robbed. He was looking to bring him in and collect a reward."

"Did Grandpa tell him Jesse James was selling shoes in Seth?"

"No Johnny. He said he didn't know anything about Jesse or Frank James."

"You mean Grandpa lied!" I was shocked to know that Grandpa had lied. "Was it alright for him to lie? Ma Maw said it's a sin to even tell a little lie."

In good conscious Aunt Lydia couldn't defend telling a lie and she deferred to an old teacher's tactic with direct instruction. "Johnny, Jesse and Frank never returned, and the detective got word the brothers were robbing banks and trains out West and he left on the next train."

"Aunt Lydia, what did the people in Seth do when they needed new shoes?" I said with a worried voice.

"Johnny, I guess they took the train to Sears for shoes and lived happily ever after. Now, you need to get to sleep, we have a lot of work to do tomorrow. (Years later, I researched the James family connection and found no relationship.)

Aunt Lydia was refreshed in the morning working in the kitchen making breakfast. Mom and Ma Maw's breakfast included eggs, bacon, sometimes sausage, toast, or gravy and biscuits. Aunt Lydia had the same available choices, but made some name changes and substitutions. Scrambled eggs became "whambled" eggs, and canned Span fried brown replacing bacon. I liked "whambled" eggs and Span, and Ma Maw was mystified when I requested "whambled" egg and fried Spam for breakfast.

"Ednie, I know what Lucille was talking about!" Aunt Lydia mentioned to Grandma when she come into the kitchen. "I may need a little help keeping the boy busy today."

"Grandma Edna had spent the cool morning working the vegetable garden directly behind her house. She would move two five-gallon bucket along as she worked using one as a seat and one to hold ripe vegetables that would be prepared for dinner. She was dressed in an old long dress and wore her garden tennis shoes and sported a wide brimmed straw hat to shield from the morning sun. She would sit among the cucumber vines pulling the few weeds that she constantly battled while picking. There was never an issue of picking too much since the family was still large and anyone that come to visit went home with fresh vegetables. When growing up, I don't recall Mom or anyone else ever talking about a snake of the farm, except one-night Aunt Lydia found a black snake in the well room. The room had a concrete floor and concrete above-ground well housing. It was the first source of fresh water when the house was built and lined with local stones. A hand pump was still functional after being primed and the water from the shallow well, likely filtered Big Coal River water, was better than the red hard water available at the kitchen sink. Adjacent to the well room, a rough-cut door that led to the cellar, and likely the snake came from the cellar. Aunt Lydia credited the concrete floor as an anchor that held the house in place during the great flood. She called her brother, James, from next door and he killed the blacksnake.

"Ednie, I hear Mr. Guthrie at the door. He's going to work in the flower garden today. Maybe between the three of us we can keep Johnny busy. In Ma Maw Oma's backyard, I entertained myself playing in my dirt pile with plastic Indians, cowboys, and soldiers. Once I had a fascination with a toy concrete mixer, and Pa Paw searched every toy store in Cincinnati, Ohio, until he found one to bring home on a Friday evening.

Ma Maw Oma's porch had potted flowers, but at Bloomingrose the side yard, and both the front yard of Aunt Lydia and Grandma's houses was covered with flowers. Aunt Lydia employed an army of men and women painting, cleaning, and working in the flowers and the house throughout the spring and summer. Mom said a flower garden was always at Bloomingrose, and the family's love of flowering plants may have suggested the name Bloomingrose, but cut flowers were never taken from the garden and arraigned in the house.

"Johnny, Mr. Guthrie will show you what weeds to pull. Stay close to him." Mr. Ray Guthrie was a retired miner needing extra cash and something to keep busy. He enjoyed working with the Midkiffs; I don't recall anyone have anything negative to say about the family.

"Johnny, stay in the shaded area and work in the snapdragons," Mr. Guthrie instructed, hoping I could keep out of trouble until lunch.

The snapdragons were as entertaining as plastic Indians, and I focused on running my fingernail down every seed pod seam, releasing popped seeds across the shady end of the flower garden.

"Johnny it's time for lunch. Lucille said you liked bologna sandwiches, but today you're having a fried Spam sandwich on toast with mayonnaise and a white onion." She looked down at her snapdragon, and it was obvious all the seeds had been released from their pods. She could understand why Mrs. Jordan sometimes requested divine intervention. "Why Johnny, we're going to have a garden of snapdragons next year."

The evening was a repeat of the evening before, that began with a plea to go to sleep. "Johnny, you had a busy day pulling weeds in the garden. You should be sleepy!" Aunt Lydia sighed.

"I worked hard in the snapdragons!" I bragged. "Tell me another story, and I think I can go to sleep."

"One story and you're going to sleep."

"Made it a story about a treasure!" I insisted.

"The Midkiff family once has a historic treasure."

"Was it some of the gold Jesse James robbed from banks and trains?"

"No, Johnny. It wasn't a treasure of gold or silver, but it was in a locked metal box that had been passed down from father to son for hundreds of years."

"Aunt Lydia can I see it. Is it in your safe behind the curtain in the hallway?"

"Johnny you're not supposed to know about my safe. Now, don't tell anyone about the safe, people might think I have money in it, and someone may try to rob me." She and Aunt Esther had safes in their homes and both feared people knowing about them and a possible robbery. Whenever I disappeared while visiting Bloomingrose, I could always be found behind the under stairs curtains attempting to unlock the safe.

"No, the box was lost years ago."

"Did Jesse James know about your safe behind the curtain?"

"No, Johnny. Jesse James didn't rob people he knew, just banks and trains."

Tell me about the treasure." I was excited since I had heard other stories about buried treasures. "What was in the chest?"

"Now you can't tell anyone about this, or we'll have people digging up our yard and the hillside." Then added, "Promise not to tell about the chest or my floor safe."

"I promise!"

"In the chest was the skull of the Indian Chief, King Philip. Grandpa Midkiff said when the box was shaken, you could hear something rattle."

"What did Grandpa do with the box? I want to open the box!"

"Johnny several others wanted to open it, and Grandpa being a Good Christ of Christ member, felt it would be like desecrating the chief's grave, and he would have no part of such a bad act." She waited baiting me. "He tied the chest with a rope and lowered it into a water well for safe keeping."

"What happened next? Can we pull the chest up?"

"No, Johnny, the rope rotted and the chest dropped into the well."

"Aunt Lydia, you mean we've been drinking skull water? No wonder your water tastes so bad! It's skull water!"

Aunt Lydia didn't foresee a problem telling the story of King Philip's skull. "Johnny we'll bring some water from Esther's tomorrow." Then she added, "Now, go to sleep. You have eggs to gather and chickens to feed tomorrow."

The next night, Aunt Lydia said, "Johnny. I know. You need a story before bed!"

"I'm ready. What story are you telling me tonight?"

"Lay back," she insisted, hoping to make a quick end to the bedtime story. "Grandpa Sutphin lived at Seth."

"Is his house still there? I asked.

"Yes, Aunt Lottie Brown, Other Mom's sister, lives there. We may go and visit her sometime this week if we find time," Aunt Lydia added, instantly regretting a promised trip.

"I can't wait to visit Aunt Lottie. I remembered Other Mom when she was sick and in Aunt Lydia's downstairs bedroom, which was a passageway to the front of the house. Its only convenience was it was adjacent to the only bathroom. The farmhouse was typical, with a front living room connected to a similar front parlor always locked and used for family wakes. The small connecting hallway opened onto the front porch and against the solid wall a pay phone was located. Like at Brushton, one phone served the entire community, and everyone in Bloomingrose memorized the phone number 13K14 as their personal number. Before the G W Midkiff's General Merchandise closed, an extension phone line was in place for the public's convenience during business hours.

Aunt Lydia continued, "When the flood came in 1916, the water came up just like here at Bloomingrose. The family wasn't as fortunate as Grandpa Midkiff, since their barn was closer to their home and was taken away with the flood."

"Like Grandpa's store building and the Baptist Church at Peytona," I added since knowing the story by heart. The flood of 1916 was more relevant to old folks than Noah's biblical flood. "Did they run for the hills like Ma Maw Oma?"

"They did! They lost everything in the barn. In a cabinet drawer, Grandpa had hidden a deed for Manhattan Island from the Indians. It was written on sheep skin." (I always wondered how the Midkiff came up with the King Philip and the deed to

Manhattan stories. They were all master story tellers. The family could have been living on 5th Avenue if not for the flood of 1916.)

"Was Grandpa sad to lose his barn?" I asked not realizing the fortune lost.

"He was more upset losing his casket he had stored in the barn."

I didn't understand someone having their casket stored in the barn and asked, "Aunt Lydia, do you have your casket in the barn?"

"Why Johnny! I'm not planning to die anytime soon!"

"Well when you do, I want your house!"

"Johnny! Go to sleep, it's been a long week! You're got eggs to gather and chicken to feed tomorrow." Then added, "Lord! Give me strength!"

Chapter 6
Back Porch Cardinals

"Ted, why are you spending so much time on the back porch?" Ma Maw Oma called from the kitchen while she was working frying pork chops for Saturday night's supper. The back porch to their Brushton home was an add-on, providing little more than protection from the rain.

"Oma, Johnny's trying out his new PF Flyers, seeing how much faster he can run to the end of the yard and back." My new shoes bought in Charleston did add to my speed, but my race was used to cover for Pa Paw's love for the St. Louis Cardinals. "Now, Johnny this time touch the tree trunk in Brother Lakin's yard." The extended track was intended to extend time on the back porch.

"Ted, what so interesting besides Johnny's new shoe on the back porch?" Ma Maw was a no-nonsense person, she could get excited over a camp meeting, church revival, perfect pie crust, but never a spectator sport.

"Oma, Johnny and I are listening to the cardinals. There's a whole flock in the back yard!"

"Ted, keep quiet not to frighten them away." Ma Maw called using a softer voice.

"Oma, I'm being real still. Just stay in the kitchen so Johnny can hear the birds at play."

Pa Paw was an avid closet St. Louis Cardinal's fan, and while I was scanning the Sunday comics, he would slip away to read the sport's page of the Charleston Daily Mail. Ma Maw would have been enraged knowing he was reading about baseball and not thinking about the preacher's morning sermon. If she had known of his secret obsession, the newspaper would have been cancelled. No comic strip reading for me and sports page Pa Paw.

Ma Maw's kitchen radio was only tuned to religious programs, with an occasional news report. Listening to a sports event was unheard of. When hand-held transistor radios became available, Pa Paw had one that he held to his ear while on the back porch, listening to Cardinal games. He would listen long enough to catch the score and follow up on game details in the sport's page. He managed to keep his radio a secret by hiding it in the car trunk, and I knew to keep the secret. It was obvious when the World Series was being played: he spent extra time peeping at the newspaper and would make trips to our house to catch ten minutes of TV time with Dad watching the Series.

"Johnny, keep your eye on the ball," he instructed before pitching a softball to me standing before a makeshift backstop of Ma Maw's wash house. He came up with a bat, glove, and ball without my knowledge, since I preferred toys. I would hit the pitched ball, and he would chase it across the yard. He hoped to encourage my interest in baseball, but I never took a great interest beyond playing in the back yard.

The community lived for baseball. Men followed favorite teams and Pa Paw's interest in the Cardinals came from his fascination with Dizzy Dean. Many followed the Yankees and the Cincinnati Reds, the closest National League team. Ma Maw's brother, RP (Giggs) Hudson, was so enamored with the sport he attended a World Series game in New York. Men would be invited on Sunday to watch the Series on a TV set atop the standing furnace on the dry-good side of Hudson's Big Star Store. TV antennas were in many back yards and mounted on rooftops. But the community store showing offered sport enthusiasts an opportunity to see the game. Pa Paw and I slipped through the rear door so he could take in a little of the game. Ma Maw was led to believe we were taking a walk to the old Wirehouse.

Softball and baseball were important activities at Nellis Elementary where three games were played on different sections of the large playground, and a volleyball game was enjoyed by non-baseball students. Basketball was a seasonal sport played in the gym and during PE class. The communities sponsored summer league ball teams when another baseball enthusiast, Ed Cain, coached and transported players to games. Summer evening in Brushton were spent riding bikes and playing hide-the-belt, (similar to capture the flag) a chase game involving the finder of a hidden belt chasing players to base while swatting them with the found belt. (It could become quiet physical.)

"Ted, I don't see any cardinals out the window. Are you sure you're not mistaken?" Ma Maw called from the kitchen. "Supper will be on the table in a jiffy."

"Oma, they're all gone now." He replied as he turned off his pocket-size transistor radio and placed it on the high porch shelf attached to the open rafters. You would think the birds were all snipes disappearing so fast!" Pa Paw said while shooing me into the kitchen. "Johnny, take your new shoes off and go wash up for supper."

"Pa Paw, what's a snipe? I don't think I ever seen a snipe."

As he helped me remove my shoes he started to tell me about snipes. "Ted, don't get started with a tall tale! Supper's on the table." Ma Maw interjection hurried us to the table, because punctuality was a personal "Commandment."

"Johnny, we'll find a snipe in our bird book after supper." A snipe was a real game bird, but rarely taken unlike quail. Many believed the snipe was a fictitious creature, either an animal or a bird that practical jokers would use on inexperienced hurters. The unsuspecting target of the prank would be given a burlap sack to hold open to wait for a snipe driven towards the bag. Eventually, he'd become aware of the lark after lonely hours in the woods.

"Pa Paw, let's look at the bird book" I had an assortment of identification books for rocks, insects, snakes, trees, and birds. Pa Paw liked locating an unknown bird and then identifying it. Once we came across an American Bittern, a bird Pa Paw had never seen. It was for a while as much a mystery as the flying saucer we spotted crossing over Brushton on a dark summer Saturday night.

"Pa Paw, I didn't see any cardinals in the back yard." I commented while thumbing through the bird book.

"Why, Johnny, I'm surprised! I could hear them all the way from St. Louis!"

Chapter 7
Hunting Pa Paws

"Oma, when we get home, Johnny and I are going up Kinder's Branch to hunt pa paws. If we don't go today, Mrs. Garrison and Dorothy will leave the trees bare!" Pa Paw Ted informed his wife as we rode back from our Saturday shopping trip to Charleston. Pa Paw had even passed up stopping at the union hall to save time since dark came fast to the narrow hollow that bordered the abandoned ARMCO golf course above Brushton.

"Ted! How could old Mrs. Garrison and Dorothy get all your pa paws? You're exaggerating again!" Ma Maw when into a sermon about how important it was to always tell the truth. "No wonder, Ted. I don't know when to believe Johnny and when he is pulling my leg."

Pa Paw, for once, was giving an accurate account of Mrs. Garrison and her old maid daughter, Dorothy. Last year, we walked to our hidden pa paw patch, and the women were already there. Dorothy was high up in the branches of a pa paw tree. Before we saw them, Dorothy was calling to her mother, "Mommy, I don't think this branch is strong enough to hold me."

Mrs. Garrison was heard to reply, 'Dorothy, you're not that high! I see several more pa paws within your reach."

The treetop daughter responded in a pleading voice, "but Mommy, I fear I'm going to fall!"

"Ma Maw!" I interjected. "Mrs. Garrison

screamed at me, 'Johnny don't look up! Dorothy's up in the tree wearing a dress.'"

"Johnny, I hope you listened to Mrs. Garrison!" Ma Maw used a strong hopeful voice. "Ted, why am I just hearing about this?"

Our encounter would have passed Ma Maw's scrutiny until I added Mrs. Garrison's warning. "Ted! You two can't even go pa paw picking without running into trouble!" Then added a dishearten threat. "Am I going to have to go pa paw picking with you?"

"Oma, I believe we are safe; the Garrisons are going to miss pa paw picking since Mrs. Garrison took a fall and is confined at home."

"Ted, I guess I can trust you two back in the woods. But I don't want any foolishness."

"Ma Maw, can I still climb the pa paw trees?" I asked, thinking Ma Maw had been upset with worry over Dorothy chanced falling from the tree.

"Well, as long as you don't climb too high and you're not wearing a dress."

"Ma Maw, why would I have a dress on? Is tree climbing easier wearing a dress?"

"Johnny! You and Ted, along with Mrs. Garrison and Dorothy are going to be the death of me!" Ma Maw closed the topic and resumed her habit of reviewing Sunday's cited scripture.

Kinder's Branch was the first branch off Brush Creek, and its head was directly across the mountain from Nellis. Along the right, for the distance of the narrow valley, a truck mine worked the same Nellis coal seam that had scarred the hollow with break outs, which allowed fresh air passage and an escape route.

"Johnny, walk behind me. I'll cut a pass through the brush," Pa Paw instructed me. The creek flowed year-long, meandering over small sand bars and rocks. Close to the mouth of the hollow, water catapulted over an 8-foot waterfall. The layer of resistant bedrock, like the seams of coal, lay under the surface exposed only at outcrops or where water erosion cut deep into the hollow's floor. Each side of the valley below the waterfall was a miniature gorge as a result of the retreating bedrock. At the left side of the falls, large rocks were inclined that were once the foundation for a logging road. The timber industry had thrived, for fifty years, until the last of the forest was cut, as evidenced by abandoned timber roads, old lumber mill sites, the absences of large timber, and remnants of rotting stumps.

Kinder's Branch was Dad's favorite location for hunting crawfish and lizards, two of his favorite fishing baits. It was the closest healthy creek. The larger and closer Brush Creek was void of anything living as a result of the acid water runoff from the Nellis mines and the Ridgeview and Nellis slate dumps. Regardless of the amount of water flow, the Brush Creek's bank and bottom was stained red. I recall seeing only one water snake in Brush Creek, and it, like the creek's rocks, was tinted red. Minnows were absent in Kinder's Branch due to the small pools of water and totally absent in Brush Creek. When Dad decided to bait with minnows, we trapped or seined Camp Creek, across the mountain where the water was free-running and less polluted. In the spring, Dad fished with his all-time favorite bait, hellgrammites, larvae of the Dobsonfly. They could be found attached to the bottom of rocks in Big Coal River. Dad's fishing partners, stationed below Dad, would hold a sein, a four-foot square finely woven net attached to two upright poles, would wade the swift cold water, and Dad bravely lifting rocks, allowing the swift current to wash the larvae to be caught in the fine-weaved sein. I ran along the river bank exploring. If five hellgrammites ended up in their bait box, it was a good catch. Dad swore fish would be fighting to be taken by the elusive hellgrammite.

"It looks like a good year for pa paws," Pa Paw Ted said while scanning the native fruit trees. "Pa paws are hard to find now-a-day, but when I was a boy at Hernshaw, the valley was full of pa paws."

"Pa Paw, what happened to all the pa paws? You think black panthers ate all the pa paws?" I worried hearing stories of panthers chasing them at night when they walked home.

"No, just turtles, along with boys," he replied.

"Can I climb the tree to get the high ones?" I asked half way up the tree.

"Think you can climb as high as Dorothy?" Pa Paw said, while picking up fruit on the ground. "The Garrisons are missing a good harvest."

"That just means more for us," I proudly jested. The pa paw trees were located under the protective shade provided by hillside trees. When the hillsides were logged, the previously shaded pa paws trees, which had no commercial lumber value, wilted under the sun.

"Johnny, looks like we have filled our pail." Pa

Paw had a favorite galvanized bucket stored in the wash house used only to pick Grandma Hudson's apples and pa paws. I would drop the fruit from the treetop, often still green, to be hand caught, and Pa Paw would then place the hard fruit in the bucket, with a lining of cushioning leaves to prevent bruising. The softer fruit found on the ground were placed on the top. We would always eat some of the ripe fruit and spit the large brown seeds, which resembled the shape of a kidney bean, on the ground, hoping it would take root next spring.

At the car, Pa Paw placed the heavy bucket in the truck and separated out several green and ripe pa paws and placed them in a Big Star grocery paper bag. "Johnny. We have one stop to make before going home."

"What stop?" I hoped it would be at Sydney and Kathrine Barker's Pure Oil station at the turn-off to Brushton. Pa Paw enjoyed visiting, and while he was absorbed in St. Louis Cardinal's talk or politics, I was content drinking a Dr. Pepper and eating a Slim Jim. Ma Maw always quarreled, complaining he spent too much time talking, but it never stopped him from visiting, regardless if he was at the Big Star, the union hall, or at Red Hager's store at Rumble, or at Barker's Pure Oil station. I listened to them talk, for Pa Paw was in his element when talking with friends.

"We're going to drop off some pa paws to Mrs. Garrison and Dorothy when we pass by." The Garrisons lived up the lane from us. They were known throughout the community as walkers. Their walks often took them miles from home in search of discarded soft drink bottles they redeemed for their three-cent deposit at the Big Star store. "You can run them to their door," Pa Paw said when we stopped at their gate. "Old folks always said pa paws are good for making you feel better, and Mrs. Garrison may recover a little earlier having a taste of pa paws."

At the house, Ma Maw's pork chop were ready for the hot skillet. She delayed cooking, not knowing if her husband stopped to talk, no telling when we would make it home. "Oma, Johnny and I made a good picking of pa paws," he announced when we came from the back to the kitchen.

"Now, Ted, leave some in the house before you store the others." The yellow meat of the pa paw, similar to a banana, was susceptible to bruising, and when aging always attracted flies and small gnats. The greenest fruit would be hidden outside in a clump of high grass where they would ripen, and Pa Paw would go in the evening for a ripened treat. Mrs. Garrison soon recovered, and she and Dorothy were spotted searching the road's ditch in search of a three-cent reward. Dorothy struggled stepping down the steep ditch embankment, her only worry when the wind of a speeding coal truck might lift her dress.

"Dorothy, now, watch your dress, we don't need make a sight, with your dress above your head!"

"Oh, Mommy!" I can't hold my dress down at the same time hold my bottles!" Dorothy replied in defense. "You won't let me wear Daddy's old pants while in the ditch or even when you're making me climb pa paw trees!"

"Dorothy, there's just some things a woman shouldn't do, and wearing men's trousers is at the top of the list!" Mrs. Garrison then added, "Dorothy, look down there, you missed a Pepsi bottle. We might need to save our bottle deposit money to get you glasses!"

"Mommy, I don't need glasses, just a pair of pants!"

Chapter 8
Parable of the Christian Potatoes

"Ted slow down, we're all anxious to see Pete, Betty, and Vicki!" Ma Maw warned Pa Paw while centrifugal force pushed her from one side of the front passenger's seat of the two-tone Chevrolet then thrusted towards the center. I road alone in the back seat, entertained by the two-way talk between the two adults riding in the front. Occasionally, I would ask a question and receive a biblical response from the passengers or a tall tale from the driver. As we pushed closer to our destination of New Martinsville, West Virginia, Pa Paw continued to toy with speed, being guilty of having a heavy foot on any open straight-a-way, a rarity of the hollow and mountain roads of Boone County.

Much of the countryside was made up of family farms, and Ma Maw was equally irritated when she sighted barns painted by the Bloch Brothers Tobacco Company of Wheeling, West Virginia, advertising Mail Pouch chewing tobacco that encouraged consumers to "Treat Yourself to the Best." Before their marriage, Pa Paw had been a chewing tobacco user, and Ma Maw had converted him to Juicy Fruit gum like she converted him from a Baptist to a Pilgrim. "Just look at such waste, children are starving in Africa, and people are wasting good farmland growing the "Devil's cabbage!"

Pa Paw simply shook his head and gently patted the steering wheel while she ranted. He knew poor people sometimes had little pleasure and a good chew offered a treat; besides struggling farmers were able to supplement farm revenue with the one- or two-dollar yearly payment and the benefit of a painted barn.

Grandpa Midkiff always had a carton of Mail Pouch and often enjoyed a chew in his jaw. Miners relied on a chew while working in the mines since a lit cigarette was prohibited, and fire in coal mines was a constant hazard started by an electrical short, friction-produced sparks, or carelessness on the part of miners or mine operators.

"Johnny, did I ever tell you about 'Hoop Snakes?' Pa Paw called to the rear seat when his attention to speed was challenged by a stretch of curvy roads and Ma Maw stopped preaching.

"Pa Paw, were they called 'Hoop Snakes' because they made noise like Indians?" I responded, eager for Ma Maw to get her breath from preaching, stimulated after we had passed the cut-field of tobacco and an open air tobacco barn.

"When Indians still hunted on Big Coal River, one of my Great-great Grandpa George Jordan's family came to Toney's Branch, just below Bloomingrose to claim his land grant he was given for service in the American Revolutionary War."

"Did he know any Indian?" I questioned, since having a liking for Indian, bear, and black panther stories.

"Hunting parties still passed through and made camp at his place. He had good water, and he traded with them." (It was true an ancestor, Johnathan Jordan, received a land grant of 286 acres on Toney's Branch, and his descendants lived in a hillside house through the 1930s. The Midkiff family now owns the old homestead site. I have visited the location several times, and the steep hillside was ill suited for farming, but likely offered good hunting in the virgin woods of early 1800s.) He continued his story, "At night they would gather around their campfire and tell stories."

"Johnny! Sit back in your seat and stop pulling on the front seat!" Ma Maw warned as she was made uncomfortable by my head perturbing over the backrest of the front seat, crowding her, when a left turn in the road, forced her towards the middle of the front bench seat. "Ted do slow down, we'll be in New Martinsville before you finish your fool story." Ma Maw would have preferred Pa Paw telling Bible stories, but she remembered how Sunday school's stories (in her opinion) would suffer from inaccuracy, if left for Pa Paw to retell. She was relieved knowing I was entertained and not free to get into mischief, as she called my adventures.

"My Papa George told me about 'Hoop Snakes'; the Indian had great respect and fear for the cunning reptile."

"Were they afraid of a snake bite?" I asked, having a fear of snakes myself.

"It wasn't snake bites, but snake stings they feared." He baited me and waited for a response. Ma Maw looked up from her Bible reading likely wondering how tall Ted's tale would be.

"Snakes don't have stingers, they have fangs!" I corrected.

"Hoop snakes were one-of-a-kind snakes with a deadly stinger on their tails. They would lay up on the top of mountain ridges and watch for a passing deer in the hollow below them. When they spotted a deer, they would put their tail in their mouth making a hoop of their body. They would roll down the hillside, and, just before hitting their target they would extend their tail that looked like an arrow and strike the victim. The stringer would shoot a dose of venom into its prey." Pa Paw clapped his open hands together, with an instant release from the steering wheel, resulting in a loud clap to replicate the sound of the stinger hitting.

Ted, you nearly scarred me to death! I thought we had a blow-out!" Ma Maw scolded after nearly jumping out of her skin.

"What happened next?" I asked while standing on the rear floor hump that accommodated the driveshaft that added six-inches to my reach, over the rear of the back of the split bench seat, again crowding Ma Maw during hard left turns.

"The venom was so instant, grazing deer would drop dead with green grass still in their mouth," he added, giving a degree of credibility to his story.

"Did the family ever have a run-in with a 'Hoop Snake?'" I asked, while nearly in the middle of the front seat.

"Ted, finish your story so Johnny will have time to settle down before we get to Pete and Betty's place."

As more people moved up Big Coal, the forest was cut and big game like deer and bears decreased, along with 'Hoop Snakes.' It was rumored one old snake remained, and one day it was sunning on a top mountain ridge waiting for a passing deer. The near-blind snake spotted what it believed to be a deer and placed its stinger tail in its mouth and started rolling towards its target. When the snake though it was close enough it sprang into its arrow position and struck solid in the supposed deer."

"Did the deer drop dead still having grass in its mouth?" I asked, now squeezed in-between Pa Paw and Ma Maw in the front seat.

"The snake had missed its target and hit a small sapling, and the small tree started to swell with the effects of the poison, and within a short time was a massive oak tree, and since the big timber had been cleared the tree was cut. Old Johnathan Jordan milled the timber and build a new barn and a corral."

"Did his cows like their new home?" I inquired.

"Johnny, they liked their new home for a month or two."

"What happened? Did the 'Hoop Snake' come back?"

"No one ever saw the snake after that day, but the swelling went out of the timber as fast as it had swollen when first stung."

"What happened next?"

Pa Paw jerked his hands away from the steering wheel and closed his hands together indicating chocking. "All Johnathan Jordan's cows were chocked, even his chickens were squeezed too death. He was just happy no one was in the barn when the swelling went out!"

"Ted Jordan! Lord have mercy! You expect us to believe that story?" I was surprised Ma Maw was paying enough attention to even question the story.

"Oma, I'm just relaying what my Papa told me and his Papa had told him," he calmly replied while a smile showed on his face and we drove on towards New Martinsville.

Between talk, Ma Maw rode while listening to Pa Paw's stories or reading her Bible. My neck stretched, searching the landscape, I had made trips to Charleston, nearly every Saturday, and rode to church camp the previous August, but this adventure was our longest trip.

"Ma Maw, shouldn't we be stopping to eat lunch. I do need to go to the bathroom," I called from the rear seat. "The fried chicken will sure taste good! You make the best."

"Johnny, didn't you go behind some trees last stop?" Ma Maw questioned, then added, "I just knew this would happen Ted, you gave the boy tea when you should have been just offering him Juicy Fruit."

"Oma, Pine Grove's just up the road, and we can make a stop," Pa Paw said. "New Martinsville not much farther."

"Ted! Don't give the boy too much tea. We'll be force to stop at the next crossing for him to find a tree," Ma Maw warned. "We won't get to New Martinsville till night. "Johnny hurry along, now!"

New Martinsville was an old Ohio River town, dependent upon river economy and then the oil and natural gas production fields that lay beneath the ground of Wetzel County. Pete, Dad's brother, like many West Virginia construction workers, during the 1950s chased work around the country and found work in New Martinsville. Betty and Vicki went with Pete, and the young family rented a second-story apartment on Main Street across the street from the public car ferry.

"Pa Paw, when are we going to ride the ferry?" I impatiently asked. We had talked about riding the ferry across the Ohio since deciding to make the trip. Pa Paw was as interested in riding the ferry and used me as a reason to make the ride. Saturday morning, Pa Paw and I crossed Main Street and found the ferry closes due to high water. The Ohio was in flood and basement business were flooded. A barber shop was closed, and Pa Paw teased me by starting to walk down the steps insisting we needed haircuts. The ferry and river were the main attractions in New Martinsville, but it was my first up-close inspection of a small city. Ma Maw was excited to visit with Pete, Betty, and Vicki, and looked forward to going to Sunday church where she was familiar with the preacher.

The preacher was a large man with a commanding voice that echoed against the painted cinder block walls. "Let me tell you brothers and sisters. There are three kinds of Christians," the preacher wailed.

"Ted, give Johnny a piece of Juicy Fruit!" Ma Maw instructed. She rarely sat with us, but since her unofficial seat was at Nellis. Likely she hoped I wasn't a problem since we were visiting a new church, and she did know several members that attended camp meeting at Culloden.

The preacher's white, long sleeve shirt was soon glued to his body with sweat after five minutes of preaching. His thinning hair was pasted to his head but not untypical of the Brylcream era. "Christians are like potatoes. Some Christians are like instant potatoes, quick work, and when they leave church, they become as cold as a bowl of left-over instant potatoes." The preacher continued to talk about potatoes, and his sermon held my interest since I liked Ma Maw's mashed potatoes. "The second kind of Christian potatoes is an agitator (a play on the word, agitator, emphasizing "tator"). "An agitator receives the 'Word of God' and gets worked up with the 'Spirit,' but like the instant potato Christian, they don't have the fire in their soul!" The preacher was a fire-and-brimstone Pilgrim and baked his parable potatoes for the better portion of an hour.

"Ted give Johnny another Juicy Fruit," she indicated to him mouthing her words and by using hand gestures. It was good she always sat, at the Nellis Pilgrim Holiness Church, in front of us since I had invented a game of seeing how far I could slide on my back on the varnished pew, after pushing off from the bench's side support. Pa Paw always made sure song hymnals were placed in their back pew holders to prevent a disruption. The other members encouraged my diversionary activity by leaving our pew empty. The sermon held my attention, and I looked forward to Ma Maw mashed potatoes with brown chicken gravy after church. Ma Maw wasn't the exception selecting a seat away from their spouse, Brother Justice always sat in front of Pa Paw, and perhaps it was their wish to be alone rather than the Sister's wish. Brother Justice was a reverse image of his wife. She was short and heavy and he was tall and lean. She was very expressive when the "Spirit" was with her, and he was very reserved with an "Amen" being his only utterance. He was exceedingly hard-of-hearing, having hearing aids inserted into his ears.

He favored his right ear that perturbed farther from his head that was trained by his supporting right hand that acted like a hearing megaphone. He listened attentively to every word from the pulpit and the music. Brother Justice had worked the Nellis Mines from its beginning to near it closing. His height was likely a challenge for him working the 5-foot coal seam of No. 2 Gas; perhaps he worked in the noisy preparation plant and that lead to his failed hearing.

"The third Christian potato is the hot potato. Have you ever cut into a hot baked potato? The heat remains until the last bite is taken and that is the kind of "Potato Christian" we all need to become! The heat of the 'Spirit' remains with us till we come for another serving of 'God's Word!'"

I am unaware of the effect of the potato sermon upon the congregation of New Martinsville, but I often reminded Ma Maw and Pa Paw of the "Agitator" while eating potatoes in their Brushton kitchen. It's now easy to understand why Jesus used Parables to teach the masses. Although a stretch to make potatoes symbolic compared to olive branches, fig trees, or palm branches the "Parable of the Christian Potatoes" has remained with me for nearly 60 years. (I would have also remembered the ferry ride.)

Chapter 9
The Missionary's Wife

"Sister Jordan, I want to thank you and Brother Jordan for putting up the young missionary and his wife during the revival." Brother Ross, the Nellis Pilgrim Holiness preacher, thanked Ma Maw at the close of Wednesday night's prayer meeting. "They will arrive Friday, and Martha and I will bring them down to your house," he added.

"Brother Ross, Ted and I are so happy to be able to help. It's a God-send to have a man-of-God and his wife staying with us." Usually visiting preachers stayed at the parsonage, or prosperous traveling preachers pulled a small camping trailer behind their car, and connected trailer utilities to either the church, the parsonage, or in the driveway of a member. But Brother Ross' large family precluded an extra bedroom for long-term visitors.

"Remember, you and your family are joining us for Sunday dinner," Ma Maw Oma reminded their preacher. The visiting missionary and his wife would be guests for dinner at different church member's homes during their stay. The fare would be the standard variety of chicken, pork, or a beef roast. Every wife had a desert she was known for, and the variety was endless. Ma Maw was famous for anything she made ranging from apple pie made from Grandma Hudson's apples to her latest favorite: Paradise Cake. Her new desert was lined with vanilla wafers, filled with a mixture of crushed pineapples in banana pudding, and topped with whipped cream.

"We road back to Brushton and listened to Ma Maw's long list of what she still needed to do before the young missionary and his wife arrived.

"Ted, I've put clean sheets on the spare bed, and I still need to go to the store to get extras."

"Oma, I thought you had already shopped," Pa Paw inquired.

"Ted, we are still planning on pounding the preacher next Saturday," Ma Maw added.

"Ma Maw, what do you have against the preacher, wanting to pound him?" I excitedly asked. One-time Ma Maw lived up to a threat to pound me and she used an egg turner when she found me in the wash house in the middle of a pile of broken glass from Pa Paw's carpenter levels. At supper, she told on me, Pa Paw scolded her saying, "Oma, no one's used them forever!"

"Johnny, I am not mad at Brother Ross. Pounding the preacher just means everyone is going to bring a pound of whatever food they have extra, like a pound of sugar or a pound of lard to help him feed his family. Brother Ross has a big family! That all that means."

I once overheard Brother Ross telling the brothers that he couldn't hang his trousers on the bedpost without having a surprise in nine months. The old men giggled, like children, and I wondered what the surprise was! Had Brother Ross lost his pants? (Thank God I didn't follow up with Ma Maw about Brother Ross' surprise. On a different occasion, I did make an inquiry to Ma Maw when I overheard old Brother Adams say he could no longer make water. "Ma Maw, why is Brother Adams worried about making water? Brushton's water is good, and we could take him a jug."

"Ma Maw was nearly speechless, "Johnny, I heard Brother Adams is doing much better. You are not to worry or ask him about it. He's very embarrassed since his house's plumbing isn't working well."

"Ma Maw, I need some paper and a pencil?" I asked after she turned off her kitchen counter radio tuned to the Hinton Tabernacle afternoon service.

"Johnny, what project are you working on? she asked.

"When Pa Paw lost Old Gyp, we made signs to nail on telephone posts all over Brushton."

"Johnny, Old Gyp came home, and we don't need to make signs for a missing dog," Ma Maw reasoned.

"Ma Maw, it's for Brother Edward. I heard him tell Pa Paw he'd lost his manhood. I thought we could help him by putting up some signs asking if anyone's seen his manhood."

Again, she was near speechless just saying under her breath, "Jesus have mercy on us!" Followed by her plea, "Jesus give me strength!"

Once the preacher and Sister Ross made a surprise visit to Ma Maw's house after crossing the railroad tracks after shopping at the Big Star. She was having the front bedroom painted, and the mattress was in the living room floor. When Brother Ross came in she was so embarrassed to have her home in disarray and an un-sheeted mattress in the front doorway. "Preacher, you want to go to bed?" Ma Maw Oma asked the preacher is an attempt to distract from her untidy living room.

After the preacher's visit, it was time for Pa Paw to fun his uptight wife. "Oma, Sister Ross nearly fell on the mattress in shock when you asked her husband if he wanted to go to bed." He held a straight face and waited for Ma Maw shocked reply.

When it sunk in, near hysterics, "Oh, Lord have mercy! What have I said to the preacher?"

"Well, Oma! You asked the preacher right in front of Sister Ross, Johnny, and me if he wanted to go to bed?"

"Ted! I did no such thing! Now, you and Johnny get that mattress back in the bedroom before someone trips on it. I don't know why I let you talk me into painting the bedroom!" Ma Maw insisted.

"Sister Jordan, I have Brother and Sister Cox, your houseguests for the next week," Brother Ross said at the doorway to the Jordan home.

"Sister Jordan, you have a lovely place. Thank you for putting us up. We'll try not be much of a bother." The missionary's young wife said, making all the necessary formalities. The couple graduated from the Cincinnati School of Divinity to become missionaries to Africa after receiving a calling from God. Most churches wanted seasoned preachers, not beginners.

"Let me show you to your room. You may need to rest up before supper."

"Sister Jordan, Simon can put our bags in the room. I would enjoy just visiting. So few of the villagers spoke English, it was like living in silence all the time," the thin woman said. She was a typical young wife of a fundamental minister wearing a dress that's hem was below her knees, her hair was pinned in a tight bun on the back of her head, and she was unadorned with jewelry, except for a small wristwatch with a black nylon strap.

"Sister Cox, tell us about Africa. I haven't been much farther than New Martinsville on the Ohio River. Now Ted went to Belgium during the war, but he doesn't have much to say about his travels." Ma Maw encouraged the conversation while serving coffee and apple pie.

"Sister Cox, are little children starving in Africa?" I asked, since always being asked to clean my plate as children in Africa would be happy just to have a bowl of pinto beans.

"Johnny, don't bother Sister Cox when you know the answer," Ma Maw added.

"Johnny, there are a lot of hungry people and a lot of sick people. When I was growing up over on Mud River, my family was poor and a lot of people were suffering from want, but nothing like what we saw in Africa. Why, the poorest Mud River family was rich compared to the village where we were assigned," Sister Cox said, then sipped her coffee. "Sister Jordan, it's nearly a sin to take pleasure in a hot cup of coffee compared to what so much of the world lacks."

Ma Maw was surprised at the missionary's wife's thoughts towards a hot cup of coffee and often the Brushton homemaker spoke without thinking.

"Sister, its Maxwell House Coffee."

"Johnny, go outside and play." Ma Maw suggested hoping to avoid me bringing up feeding Old Gyp turkey liver and gizzards when children were hungry in the world.

"Ma Maw, I want to stay." I have a hundred questions for Sister Cox," I answered as I moved closer to Sister Cox.

"Sister Jordan, I don't mind Johnny's questions. There was always so much noise around with wild animals in the bush, children crying at night, and cattle moving in the pins; Johnny's questions are like the pleasure of a good cup of Maxwell House. Simon and I had just one another in the Bush. I cared for the physically needy, and Simon cared for the spiritual needs of the village."

"Sister Cox, don't be startled by the train; it'll soon pass through town. Why we give it a never mind; it's just part of life here." Ma Maw apologized for the noise of the passing train fifty feet from her living room. The house quavered with the passing. Everyone sipped coffee and waited for the train to pass.

"Sister Jordan, I give the train a never mind. Even during the night, there was so much noise you could have shouted hallelujah at the top of one's lungs, and no one would have been made aware."

It was a rare occasion to have dinner in the dining room on a Thursday evening, but it was exceedingly rare to have house guests who were not family. At times, far away family members would come for a visit to Grandma Hudson's or a sister from Oklahoma would come for a stay with Aunt Francis Hudson, but Ma Maw Oma had few outside guests. Equally rare was to have a beef pot roast served on a weeknight.

The missionaries slept in the front bedroom

that was used when I spent time there. Typically, we stayed up late and always rose early, but the guest retired to bed early, and Ma Maw forcefully suggested we follow their example so not to disturb their rest. Ma Maw made a bed on the living room couch for me.

Morning breakfast was served in the kitchen, and Ma Maw was quiet to prepare Pa Paw's lunch box for work and sent him out the backdoor to prevent disturbing the front bedroom missionary couple. Soon, I was at the kitchen table, aroused by the smell of fried bacon.

"Johnny, are you still sleepy? she asked, seeing me rubbing my eyes.

"Ma Maw, Sister Cox kept me awake most of the night, moaning and groaning. I thought about going to check on her, but I was so tired," I innocently reported.

"Johnny, Sister Cox just has a bad case of asthma! Don't you as much as mention it to her or anyone." Then Ma Maw added, "Johnny it would embarrass her to think she kept you awake with her hard breathing and moaning."

"Ma Maw, I thought Sister Cox was going to die she was struggling so," I added while continuing to rub sleep from my eyes.

"Let me fix you some gravy and biscuits. It's your favorite." Ma Maw hoped to keep me busy eating, and preventing me from asking too many questions." She always kept an aluminum container on the stove top she poured bacon grease from her hot skillet. A retractable strainer separated small pieces of bacon from the oil. Bacon grease was used whenever she needed a flavoring oil, and Crisco shortening was used when a large amount of shortening was needed for frying chicken.

"Johnny, we are going to let our guests sleep in late. Stay out of the house today so not to disturb them." She had given quick thought to a plan of keeping me busy and avoiding questions. "I want you to play in the back yard. I will bring you a sandwich for lunch on the back porch."

"Ma Maw, I've never eaten on the back porch! Am I going to eat supper outside?" I was puzzled, since Ma Maw was a stickler for not changing her daily pattern.

"Johnny, I think you'll stay at your house tonight since the couch isn't good for your back."

It was a long trying week for Ma Maw. She had anticipated a week equal to time spent at the church camp meeting at Culloden. Sister Cox's nightly asthma attacks had pressed the hope from realization.

The revival closed the following Saturday night, a special night for the missionary to use keepsakes brought from Africa to display and center his sermon on. The open area fronting the alter rail what appeared to be a brown multi-colored rug spread out. Brother Cox explain the rug was a tanned snake skin. I was fascinated and Pa Paw fought to hold me in the pew.

Just before the altar call, Brother Cox announced from the pulpit, "Nellis friends, thank you for your kindness. Brother and Sister Jordan's hospitality was a true blessing we will never forget. This morning I received word, Gladys and I have been offered a church at Pleasant Valley up in Marion

County, and we have accepted."

The congregation chorused in celebration of "Amen." Several members stood in response to the good news. An "Amen "was the highest form of respect, and even the most moving of Brother Lakin's singing would be saluted with "Amens." After the altar call, the revival closed, and Pilgrims passed through the church door, offering a farewell greeting and God's blessings for the missionary and his wife. Sister Kinder was heard to be planning to pound the new preacher, since they were just starting housekeeping. Ma Maw was excited about the preacher's pounding and talked about it on the way home to Brushton. I rode in the back seat and listening to the conversation.

Ma Maw was pleased the revival was successful and said, "Ted, the 'Spirit' was strong at the service. Do you think when Brother and Sister Cox settle we can make a trip to deliver what our brothers and sisters put together?"

"Oma, I think it would make a good trip," Pa Paw added.

"Ma Maw. Before we go visit Sister Cox, we need to go to the store. I was telling Aunt Francis about Sister Cox's moaning and groaning all night long, keeping everyone awake, with her attack of asthma, and she showed me a box of pills for asthma. I think we should get that for Sister Cox in the pounding so Brother and Sister Cox can get a good night's rest."

"Johnny, I don't think asthma pills will help Sister Cox," Pa Paw said without thinking of the consequences of opening the subject.

Ma Maw interrupted, hoping to move the conversation away from Sister Cox's sleeping habit. "Ted, I don't think I would have sleep a wink knowing that snake was up under the bed!"

"Ma Maw, do you thing that was what was bothering Sister Cox? All the noise she was making. I think she was trying to get away from the snake!" I said, hoping that Sister Cox wasn't suffering from an ailment and rather just fear of a snake.

Pa Paw slowed the car, giving time for the subject to come to a hilarious end. He knew his wife would try to close with a reasonable solution, knowing I would make inquires to the Pilgrim brothers and sisters at the most inopportune time.

"Ma Maw, would you have been moaning and groaning making all that noise and keeping everyone awake if a big snake was coming at you?" I questioned.

"Well Oma, now tell us, would you be in the same position as the missionary's wife if confronted with a big snake?"

"Ted, I don't want to hear another word! You and Johnny get home and make hot coco and cinnamon toast and get to bed!" Ma Maw said, hoping the subject was closed. "Lord, give me strength!" was her final word.

Chapter 10
Wild Ride in Rumble

"Pete you sure the brake working?" His younger brother asked.

"We've made this ride a hundred times," came reassuring words. The gang of boys had walked from Brushton to the site of the old Coal River Collieries at Rumble, West Virginia. The mining company was unique in the coal fields of southern West Virginia, unlike the ARMCO mines at Nellis owned by the American Rolling Mills of Middleton, Ohio, to supply their steel mills with metallurgical coal, the Rumble mines was owned by the labor union of the Brotherhood of Locomotive Engineers (BLE) as an investment.

The mine facility was state-of-art in the 1920s when built. People bragged it was the largest tipple in the country, spanning the valley and having head houses on both side of the mountain to access coal seams. Like at Nellis, a dead-end spur rail line was built, branching from the C&O Railroad at Ashford, where a large Y turn-a-round was included at the mouth of Lick Creek to accommodate steam engines limited ability to travel in reverse for long distances. The track snaked up the narrow valley to the tipple pushing empty cars beyond the tipple to dead-end at Casey's Fork and used gravity to feed cars under the coal chutes located under the tipple. Company housed were built to house workers in Lower Rumble and Upper Rumble coal camps, and a company store was built along with building dedicated to repair.

Unlike ARMCO, the mining company at Rumble provided no support for public schools, churches, or recreational activities.

Mine production was limited at Rumble due to continual labor disputes between The United Mine Workers (UMW) union and the mine owner that, in reality was the union of locomotive engineers. The final blow came with the Great Depression, when the limited demand for coal closed the Rumble mine, and the equipment that could be salvaged was sold. The slate dump that rose in a short valley near the tipple was small compared to Nellis and Ridgeview, which operated at least three times the amount of time as the Coal River Collieries.

The boys had worked hard pulling the mine car back up the in-grade past the head house located adjacent to the sealed mine entrance. Ropes were used like harnesses had once been hitched to mine mules pulling out mined coal. A running push would send the mine car loaded with six boys down the incline, and the makeshift brake, made of a four by four strapped against the car's side, would be pulled to press against the steel wheel to slow the car before it ran out of track.

"Pete, pull the brake!" Jake Nelson screamed close to the end of the track, then the first to jump from the runaway car. Extreme force was applied to the four by four and the cracking sound when the brake broke was enough warning for everyone to make a frantic jump.

Someone screamed, "Jump now or die!"

The hillside was littered with tumbling bodies of boys that feared the end of track more than abrasion resulting from the collision against slate strewn along the mountainside. Another cried a last warning, Jerry! Jump!" Jerry Hudson was younger than his friends and somehow failed to make the jump and road to the end of track.

"Jerry! Jerry!" The group called in unison as they chased down the steep hillside. "Panicked someone screamed, "What are we going to tell his mother?"

The friends expected the worst when they upturned the mine car stopped by a tree, Jerry rolled from the car and asked, "When's the next ride?"

"Johnny, this isn't a good idea," Eddie warned as we pushed our bikes up the incline. After Nellis, Ridgeview, and the Orlandi mines closed, numerous small truck mines opened to exploit the remaining seams of coal. The truck mines operated under the ownership and management of local owners that had worked in the mines their entire life coming from families with a history of mining. Many early homesteads opened backyard seams of coal used for house coal. At Bloomingrose, Grandpa Midkiff mined the five-foot seam of Eagle behind his home to use in his house. Upriver the family owned thirty-acres of hillside above Maxine where the Eagle seam was easily accessible, and a neighbor, Mr. Dobbs, was working it during the night. Aunt Lydia got word of the theft and took action, along with her Poppy's pistol and settled the issue. Mr. Dobbs' pull cart was confiscated by Aunt Lydia and was stored under the corn crib as her trophy. When asked about it, when we walked by to gather eggs and feed the chickens and pigs, she would always stop, place her hands on her hips, and say, "Mr. Dobbs didn't take any more Midkiff coal after I made a visit!"

The truck mines were largely automated with loaders gathering the coal broken by shooting with dynamite and blasting caps. A continuing caravan of coal trucks lumbered down the narrow two-lane road crossing the mountain and dumping their loads at the Marmet river terminal.

"Eddie, look there's a man by the bulldozer; we can ask if we can watch." Encouraged, we moved closer to the mining operation. The 36-inch Powellton Seam located near the middle of the top half of the mountain was being mined, and a metal chute ran down the mountain where the mined coal was loaded into trucks.

"Sure, you can watch. Move closer to see better!" The worker said, then added, "When you hear a loud buzzer sound, the coal will be coming down the chute."

Shortly, the buzzer sounded followed by a growing roar of rocks banging against the metal retaining walls of the chute. We should have realized the hazard of our up-close point of observation since the attendant scurried downhill at the sound of the buzzer. The noise of the avalanche of coal was deafening, and when the coal shot free from the end chute, the sound resembled a mortar impact. A black wall of coal dust instantly engulfed us. "Run!" Eddie screamed. Before the warning buzzer we noted a coating of coal dust high in the limbs, but failed to make a connection. Our fast exit failed to outpace the chocking cloud of black dust. Eddie and I were as black as miners working at the face after a double shift. We passed the attendant that had wearing a wide grin, proud of his prank.

"That's the last time I'll let you talk me into being where we're not supposed to be!" Eddie coughed while spitting black. I had nothing to say.

I hoped to keep my bad experience a secret, because if Dad was told of the prank played on me, he would have been like Aunt Lydia taking her Poppy's pistol to settle with Mr. Dobbs. The bulldozer operator would have been blacker than Eddie and me if Dad had known.

Dial soap doesn't cut coal dust. "Johnny! My bathtub a mess. What is this black ring around my tub?" Ma Maw Oma angrily inquired. "It's going to take a whole can of Comet!" I was luck she had never lived with a coal miner, and I convinced her I had followed to close to a coal truck while riding my bike.

Coal dust was in every crease of my body and would have eventually wore off with time, but Mom was taking me to Dr. Glover's for a physical to go to scout camp.

"Johnny you're mighty young to be mining coal!" Dr. Glover commented after a quick examination and noting the black creases of coal dust. Mom and Ma Maw would have died of embarrassment if they had known.

I explained what happened. "Well Johnny, did you and Eddie learn a lesson?" he inquired while working to conceal his amusement.

I shook my head in the affirmative leaving a ring of coal dust on the examination table.

"Just use plenty soap and hot water with a wash

cloth. In time you won't be a coal miner," he finished and signed I was physically fit to attend scout camp. If I'm ever diagnosed with black lung, I can attribute it to living alongside a railroad track and my coal mining experience at the truck mines at Laurel Branch below John's.

    Years later, the truck mine at Laurel Branch and above the Brushton Golf Course were closed. The downhill coal chute had been salvaged for junk, but the imprint of a coal remained scattered on the ground where Eddie and I became coal miners. The mine opening had been closed, but an imprint remained of a long cut against the mountainside. Like at the golf course mine site, an abandon school bus remained, once used as storage for mine supplies. When Larry and I explored the bus, we came across blasting caps used to detonate blasting power after tamped into drilled holes at the mine face. Once again the Pilgrim's prayers for "Jesus' protection" shielded us from our foolishness.

Chapter 11
Trick-or-Treat

"Johnny do you have your costume on?" Pa Paw asked while finished supper dishes.

"Do you think anyone will know Zorro is me?" I excitedly asked while adjusting my mask that had one-way glass as eye cover. Zorro was the Sunday evening TV show that was a have-to-see for me.

"Ted, just like I warned, Johnny has stopped going to Sunday evening service so he can watch Zorro on TV." Ma Maw scolded.

Television had become an important past-time during the 1950s. We weren't the first family to have a television set, but we were among the most avid viewers. Antennas were attached to nearly every rooftop or in every backyard. Three stations were available, and to change stations often required someone to repositions the antenna in a more favorable direction.

The Pilgrims and the Church of God (Holiness) were the long holdbacks against television, but the Church of Christ couldn't find an endorsement nor condemnation in the New Testament. Grandpa Hudson watched the news and weather reports and Grandma Hudson was Brushton's biggest fan of TV wrestling programs. Dad was a late- night viewer, watching the Tonight's Show with Jack Parr. Mom tolerated TV but never a regular viewer.

"Oma, we'll be back in an hour or so."

"Ted. I'll be here waiting. Several cars have already dropped kids off in front of the store. It's going to be a busy Halloween." Ma Maw was indifferent to the holiday, considering its pagan history. Local churches were neutral, but if the Pilgrims had been instructed from the pulpit, Halloween would have been eliminated. She enjoyed handing out treats and visiting with neighbors that stood behind the masked visitors. Pa Paw enjoyed Halloween as much as I did. He visited with people and laughed and played with kids. The few families that refused to participate locked their front gates and turned off their porch light. Everyone knew it was a dry hole for Halloween treats at the darken houses.

"Johnny, we'll start next door at the Justice's." The house was a near duplicate of Ma Maw's home. A round lighted globe on the porch ceiling greeted trick-or-treaters and Mary Justice answered the knock on the door. She, like Ma Maw stayed manning the front door and greeting scrambling kids, with a hand out for a candy treat, while her own children participated in filling bags with treats. "Trick-or-treat!" I screamed with excitement.

"Well little boy, who are you dressed as?" Mary asked. "I know. You're on TV Sunday night. Why, you're Zorro!" Mary dropped a handful of candy in my bucket. "Evening Ted. Having a good time?" It was a joke; she knew he was having a great evening visiting with everyone and funning around.

Corn night was practiced the night before, where kids would put soap on windows and practice pranks. Roads would be blocked, requiring a constant vigil of sheriff's patrol traveling the road from the head of Len's Creek to the foot of Ridgeview Mountain.

Pranksters imagined being chased by deputy sheriffs and fanaticized pistol shots fired into the air to disperse revelers.

"Ma Maw, we got a whole bucket of treats. This is better than Easter!" Halloween was a scheduled holiday everyone looked forward too except those Brushton residents that left their porch light off.

Unlike sanctioned holidays, a celebration was announced with every heavy snow. At times, heavy snow would down power lines, and Brushton would return to kerosene lanterns for light and to rely on natural gas to heat uninsulated houses. The houses that Grandpa Hudson built at Brushton were piped for natural gas lighting, with three-eighth-inch gas lines running across attic rafters to every room. The obsolete system was modernized with the electrification of Coal River in the 1920s. Once individual families had back yard natural gas fired electric generators to power washing machines and other modern electrical appliances. Although the forest had an abundance of timber, that could have been taken as firewood, few families heated with cords of cut timber. Company houses at Nellis were supplied with lump coal, and the houses at Brushton has triangle brick fireplaces offering an opening in the living room, dining room, and middle bedroom, designed with a shallow firebox for burning lump coal, not large enough to accommodate logs. The fireplaces had been sealed with sheetrock years ago when gas space heaters became the norm. Pa Paw and Ma Maw visited Brother Lakin and Sister Kincaid for Sunday dinner when that lived in a company house up John's Hollow. The heating system was modernized to a freestanding coal-burning furnace still dependent on lump coal, since natural gas wasn't avail. I recall the room being uncomfortably hot and dry.

Brushton continued as usually after the main roads were salted and traffic resumed. Boone County schools closed being without electricity, and we were allowed to enjoy the snow. Every neighborhood had a favorite hill for sled riding, Racine had "Racine Hill", Ashford had "Ashford Hill" and at Brushton we had "The Church House Hill."

"Pa Paw can we go up on the 'Church House Hill?' I've being waiting to try my new sled from last Christmas."

It was pathetic; when I'd get a new bike for Christmas, heavy snow would prevent riding before the spring melt, and when I got a snow sled under the tree, snow failed to visit Brushton. Grandma Hudson's yard had a good incline, but the snow was never hard packed like on the Church House Hill.

"Johnny, we can go sledding, but we'll need to be careful," Pa Paw warned. Guiding a sled down the hill was like the first time driving a car alone. At the foot of the hill, car traffic continued to travel into Brushton, and drivers took caution, realizing sledders assumed they had the right-of-way. Older boys often hitched a ride on passing cars with a tight grip on a car bumper.

While I made a hundred runs down the hill and running back to take another run, Pa Paw visited with others supervising their children. Someone would always highjack car tires to be burned to keep the frozen sledders warm. Black smoke left a dark film on everyone and was nearly as impossible to wash off as coal dust. When melted holes appeared in the hard packed snow and ice, sleds would return to backyard sheds, awaiting another holiday break.

Chapter 12
Caged Bear at Glasgow

"Johnny, we're going to see a bear. Oma's helping Mrs. Hudson make apple butter, and we're going to the junk yard at Glasgow."

"Pa Paw, why would a bear be in a junk yard? Is it the same bear that was sleeping in our apple tree?" I asked while riding in a borrowed Chevy truck. Pa Paw was determined to replace the clothesline poles in their back yard. He had bumped into a frayed wire strung from one post to the other while walking at night and nearly lost an eye.

"No. Our bear is at the Gulf station across the street from the junk yard, and we'll visit him after we get our clothesline poles. Can't have such a danger in the backyard," Pa Paw replied. He was well acquainted with the upper Kanawha River valley since working at many of the industrial sites along the river. He had worked on the Appalachian Power plant at Glasgow in 1953 and hoped the caged bear was still a service station attraction two years later.

"Johnny, get down from there!" Pa Paw called to me on top of a stack of crushed cars. He was busy talking, and I took the opportunity to explore the new playground. We found the necessary pipe for the new clothes line poles and they were strapped in the bed of the Chevy truck.

"Do we get to see the bear next?" I was eager to visit a caged bear, since my last encounter was with a free range bear. Pa Paw were bears in the wood when you were growing up?"

"When I was a boy hunting in the woods up Ring Hollow, I was standing on a ridge half way up the mountain, and all the sudden I was being hugged."

"Was it your Mama hugging you?" I wondered, think what else would hug a boy.

"I looked down and two hairy arms was holding me. I guested it to be a bear."

"Were you afraid?" Recalling my bear experience in the front yard, I was scared reaching up to pet a sleeping bear.

"I was scared, but my Dad had warned me about bears and to stand my ground and never show fear and try to surprise the bear."

"What happened next? Did you call for help?"

"No, I stayed calm and stated to turn around to face the bear face-to-face. Then I licked my lips and got them really wet and kissed the bear in its mouth."

"Pa Paw, I would never kiss a bear! What happened next?"

"Johnny, all the sudden, the bear released me, and I didn't waste time; I started running!"

"What happen? Did the bear chase you? Did you climb a tree?"

"I ran until I got to the next ridge, and I couldn't hear the bear behind me. You know they make a lot of noise running in the woods." His arms were sliding up and down the steering wheel simulating arm movement while running. "I started to slow down and still couldn't hear the bear breaking limbs and branches, so I took a chance and slowed down and looked around."

"Pa Paw, what did you see? Was the bear hot on your heals?"

"The bear was nowhere close, so I stopped running, looked back, and spotted the old she-bear back on the other ridge."

"Pa Paw what was the bear doing? Was she licking her chops getting ready to eat you?"

He lifted one hand from the steering wheel making a motion indication of "come back."

"Well, the old she-bear was motioning her arm. I think she wanted me to come back for another kiss!" He leaned back in the truck seat laughing while I duplicated his reaction of laughing at a love sick she-bear.

We found the caged bear and Pa Paw asked. "Johnny, do you think this old bear would want a wet kiss?" He said while licking his lips for another wet kiss.

"Pa Paw, we need to get home. Ma Maw needs to hang out the wash," I suggested, still having a little fear of bears, even if locked in a cage.

Rather than heading home, and it was getting close to lunch time, Pa Paw decided to make a special stop. "Johnny we have extra time, Oma's busy making gallons of apple butter and won't miss us. We're going to see the "bus on the rock."

We traveled up river to Glen Ferris, just above the Kanawha Fall at the conjunction of the Gauley and New Rivers forming the Kanawha River. Across the joined rivers was the beginning of the New River Gorge with a high rock formation fronted by the C&O Railroad skirting its bottom section. A West Virginia Department of Transportation sign gave warning, "Watch for Falling Rocks," Pa Paw pointed out.

"We're going to take lunch at the picnic tables." We always had Saturday lunch when in Charleston at the Woolworths TG&Y, but rarely did we eat when on the road. Ma Maw had made us Bologna sandwiches with mayonnaise along with several of her famous chocolate chip cookies. Pa Paw was always reverent bowing his head when Ma Maw always said grace. "Lord best our food and continue to look after us," was his to-the-point prayer. While eating, I was fascinated by the wide river, the rock cliff, and the "bus on the rock" riding on a large rock in the middle of New River.

"Pa Paw, how did the bus get out in the middle of the river?" I asked, wondering if it came in with a flood like the church bell of the Brushton Methodist Church. If a flood could move a church it could surly move an old Greyhound bus.

"Johnny, the bus is a fishing camp and was barged over and off-loaded to the rock.

"Can we go over to see the bus? Daddy would like to fish on the rock."

"We're going to have to be satisfied with just looking at it. We didn't bring a boat." We continued to eat our lunch and had ice tea and Pa Paw took coffee from his thermos. He drank coffee on the hottest summer day. "Johnny, you remember the sign we passed that I pointed out?" he asked.

"The falling rock sign?" I responded.

It was unexpected that a warning road sign would lead to a story. "Years ago Indians lived on New River. Every Indian brave was required to leave his village, and go on a quest to become a man."

"Pa Paw, am I going to have to go on a quest

before I become a man?" I was worried about bears and black panthers in the woods.

"No. When you register to vote, as a Democrat, then you become a true man." Pa Paw always had a political opinion. He and his family always worked hard, and he was an exception having a job during the Great Depression. Ma Maw was also a strong Democrat and said if Jesus was physically walking the streets of Brushton, he would be a registered Democrat. When Pa Paw talked about the Republican Party he had one stone-faced response, "They never done nothing for our family!" He often told a story of a man eating an apple during the Great Depression and a hungry man stopped the apple eater and asked, "When you're finished eating your apple can I have the core?" The apple eater replied, "What core!" He held such a dislike for President Herbert Hoover, Ma Maw was discouraged from buying a Hoover vacuum cleaner.

Pa Paw continued his story, "Early one morning, the Indian brave left his village and walked deep into the woods on his quest. After several months, the brave never returned to his village, and the council decided they needed to search for him since he was a favorite story teller to the villagers."

"How long did they search for him? Do you thing bears got him? They can get mighty hungry!"

"The tribe continued to search for him and did not found him, but they didn't give up. An old wise man suggested they put signs up to continue the search, and that's what they did. To this day they are still looking for the Indian brave with signs by the road to remind everyone to keep looking."

"Pa Paw, I haven't seen and signs!" I argued.

"Johnny, remember the sign, 'Watch for falling rocks'? Well, the brave's name was Falling Rocks, and his people are still searching for him!"

"Pa Paw, you're pulling my leg like Ma Maw says you're always doing to her!"

"Maybe so, but you saw the signs all along the road, didn't you?"

"Ted, I'm tuckered out! Mommy had three bushels of apples, and I will be pealing apple in my sleep." Ma Maw announced when we returned to her kitchen. "Mommy sent you three quarts of apple butter."

"Ma Maw, how are you going to peal apples in bed?" I asked confused, since she was a stickler for only allowing food in the kitchen and on special occasions in the dining room. "Pa Paw said we could open our own apple butter store with all the apple butter in the closet."

"Johnny, sit down on the back porch, and I'll bring you a bologna sandwich to hold you till dinner." I spent many summer eating on the back porch. Then she added after reviewing what was said, "Ted, you know we used all the apple butter! Johnny has it on toast every morning." Dad often said he couldn't eat an apple being "appled out" picking apples for Grandma Hudson while growing up. I had the same feelings towards apple butter, and eventually even Old Gyp, Pa Paw's rabbit dog, felt the same, since she no longer gulped down morning toast covered with apple butter I slipped to her.

"Johnny, I just meant I would be dreaming of apples and apple butter working in Mommy's hot canning room, most of the day" she said, attempting to reason with me.

"Ma Maw, if you're going to have a dream, are you going on a quest like Falling Rocks?"

"Ted! What is the boy talking about?" Ma Maw was still frazzled from pealing apples. She wasn't so much worn out pealing apples, but she worried about her mother and her friends working in the hot canning room.

"Ma Maw. Falling Rocks was never found after having a dream, and they put sign on all the telephone poles," I attempted to explain. Pa Paw stood back to allow funning with his tight pealed wife.

"I don't know nothing about any falling rocks."

"Ma Maw, is passing gallstones anything like falling rocks?" I questioned, beings somewhat familiar with gallstones since Ma Maw was always complaining of have a gallbladder attack, and Sister Castle passed a glass jar containing her stones around to be examined at a Wednesday night prayer meeting. Ma Maw was embarrassed when I told Sister Castle, "Her stones looked like white railroad gravel."

Pa Paw returned to Brushton every evening and worked on the new clothesline poles. One evening he dug a hole at each end of the backyard to set the posts. I helped, being a seasoned digger, spending my summer days digging in the back yard. It was unlike Ma Maw to allow a bare spot in her yard, but it was a small sacrifice considering what I would be into if not digging holes and playing in my dirt pile. Pa Paw placed a board over the holes to prevent a miss-step or the possibility of someone filling the holes with plastic soldiers and Indian braves.

That evening I tried to explain to Pa Paw to ease his worry that the hole had called my name: "Come play in the hole and see how deep it is. You can climb back out."

During the day, I slipped into the hole believing I could climb out, since I was a master tree climber. I dropped to the bottom, trapped unable to reach above the top of the fresh dug hole. "Help! Help!" I screamed but the deep hole muffled my call. My fingers extended barely above the top edge of the hole. I was unsure how much time passed, and I continued to call for help. After my calls, I heard the slam of Ma Maw's backdoor and hoped to be rescued, but no help came. I wondered if Pa Paw would post sign on Brushton telephone poles requesting, "Watch for Johnny Jordan."

Mom had told me, you could see stars during the daytime, if you were in the bottom of a well, but the only thing I could see was blue sky. "Johnny, what are you doing down in that deep hole?" Aunt Betty, Pete's wife, scolded as she looked down at the top of my head. "I kept hearing someone calling for help, I'm come to the back porch and couldn't see anyone." She bent down and took my extended fingers and rescued me. She had come out again to investigate the calls and spotted my fingers extended just above the edge of the hole.

"Johnny, you could have been lost!" He put his head in his hands. It was the most distressed I had ever witnessed him. That evening, he filled the holes to be re-dug on Saturday when we worked together setting the poles. All the Pilgrim's prayers saved me from joining all the buried plastic soldiers and

cowboy in Ma Maw's backyard and Falling Rocks, the Indian brave.

Chapter 13
Rocking in the Devil's Chair

"Old Gyp can run free; she'll not go far unless she scents a deer," then Dad added, "But that's not likely, since it would need a packed lunch to cross Boone County." In Dad's boyhood he lived in the woods and enjoyed returning to explore. The forest had greatly change from his boyhood which wasn't the case when his father, Pa Paw Ted's youth, when much of the forest was virgin. The forest was in its first stage of regrowth, when Dad roamed the hills and, now the forest was mature. Forest fires sweep through the undergrowth and leaf litter unchecked nearly every fall that were the only objection to the forest growth.

Ma Maw Oma spoke of hunting chestnuts in the chestnut grove above Peytona, which locals shared with farmers' pigs free ranging in the woods to forage until fattened for the fall kill. By the 1940s, the chestnut blight had reduced the chestnuts too isolated stands. Forests of knocked-down chestnuts trees littered the mountain side, and the sun bleached wood of dead trees was as still as a cemetery with the exception of new growth coming from rotting stumps attempting to reestablish.

"Lucille try not to get ahead of us. You're making us look bad." Dad teased Mom as she worked her way up the steep pipeline right-of-way that straight-lined to the mountain's ridge.

"Obble, you forget. We lived in the mountains behind Bloomingrose when I was a girl." At Bloomingrose the family's cows were allowed to graze in the mountains. Large predatory animals of bears and panthers, like Dad's passing deer, packing a lunch, were no long a threat. The biggest threat was when the family's bull would break loose from its pen and chase everyone into the safety of trees.

"Dad, when will we get to the 'Devil's Chair?'" I asked, while questioning what it would look like up close. The rock formation that rode the high ridge of the nameless mountain running along Big Coal River above Ashford was visible from Brushton when the trees were bare. The formation resembled a chair and was silhouetted against the setting sun. It was an odd choice of a name, since churches outnumbered beer joints and bars in Boone County. Another massive rock formation rose on Bee Mountain in Hernshaw and was known as the "Devil's Tea Table." Still another ridge top rock outcrop was called the "Devil's Spine." Locals accepted the descriptive titles without a second thought, Ma Maw said, "People always told stories of strange going-ons at the sites and it wasn't doings of Pilgrims!" She explained everything not measuring up to Pilgrim standards as a work of the Devil, and no one was climbing to the ridge tops to have church service.

Dad's dogs were excited to be out, since rabbit season was their only freedom from backyard pen. Soon, they were barking on-trail and then a different bark. Before the industrialization of the area, families were hunter-gathers, dependent upon the land for substance. The heritage continued with nearly every family having a favorite rabbit or squirrel dog. Dogs had their own language, and seasoned hunters could read their barks to determine if a dog was cold-trailing, on a hot trail, or had treed or holed their prey. Dad's dogs were universal and would chase any game. We rushed around the mountainside, as Dad was panics hearing the cries of Old Gyp. Her barks indicated trouble, and we rushed to investigate. It was early fall, and hunting season was open, but Dad was without his shotgun. The dogs had a big coon backed into a hollow tree trunk. Each dog would take a turn at snapping at the mad coon, but the coon had the advantage of three sides of protection. Many old timers were coon hunters, but I suspected coon hunting was an excuse to get out in the woods at night with friends and a community bottle of spirits. Sides of barns sported coon hides, and some families continued to eat coon, but it wasn't as common as fried chicken at Sunday dinner. Dad was given a dressed coon and Ma Maw cooked it with sweet potatoes, to kill the wild favor, in her pressure cooker. I recall the meat as being red in color and stringy; it wasn't bad, but coon was served only once.

Dad had to pull the dogs away from the holed-up coon and put them on leashes. They struggled to return to pursue their prey, while we made our way to the top ridge. The dogs continued to bark, and we were close in competition, talking about our daytime coon hunt.

Trees had taken root in the thin soil atop the "Devil's Chair," which added mystery to the rock formation. The seat portion was long, and the backside of the structure was raised, resembling a chair's back. Unseen from the Brushton, the formation was split, creating a walking passage between the seat and back portion. Larry and I raced over the outcrop exploring the eroded rock. We chalked our initials and a date, memorializing our conquest of the "Devil's Chair."

Chapter 14
Hunting Molly Moochers

"Johnny the way you go after Mary's breaded cubed-deer steak, I know you'll love fried molly moochers!" Foster Justice said to encourage me to continue our straight-up-the-hill climb.

"Foster, you sure molly moochers only grown on the high side of the mountain and not down by the river?" I questioned. I was very fit for hill climbing, but it was a challenge traveling straight up a steep incline. Forster was nearly fifty, but spry. He kept pace with me and his sons, Robert and Charlie, walking a short distance, stopping, and taking a breath, then moving on up the hill. Foster's family was traditional, enjoying the benefits of the mountain's bounty and working in nearly Charleston, like many Brushton families. They were good Methodists and Foster's father had been a local Methodist minister.

Foster always had hunting dogs penned in their back yard, ready for fall hunts. The hunts were as much a custom as going into the woods to forage for spring plants for greens. Before local stores had produce sections, family made a practice of gathering the early spring greens to supplement their greens-short diet. Locals enjoyed tender pokeweed shouts, dandelion leaves, wild onions, and mountain ramps. At Ma Maw's house, pa paws gathered in the fall was the only plants taking from the woods. It was a special spring treat to get spring leaf lettuce, radishes, and green onions from local gardeners. Our neighbor, Tunsel Barker, an expert gardener, had a hot frame box with a covering of cheese cloth, used to shield the tinder plants from the sun and hungry insects, which made the first spring harvest possible. Ma Maw would cut the lettuce and green onions then drench it with a combination of hot bacon grease, vinegar, and sugar. (Bacon grease wasn't bad for you in the 1950s.)

Mushroom hunting was restricted to only several weeks during the spring, depending upon the amount of rain and sunshine. Locals had favorite proven hunting grounds, like they had for ginseng, and it was like being considered a family member to be trusted with the secret location. The Justice family was open to collecting mushrooms or gathering garden produce on Sunday, since that considered activities with their family, not a conflict with God's commandant to keep the Sabbath holy. Ma Maw Oma's work restriction was more rigid than the Methodists', but other faiths believed to even cook food on the Lord's Day of Rest was an abomination.

"Come on Johnny, we'll soon be filling our bags with merkels." Foster encouraged. The mountainside was below the first rise behind the Methodist church house. Dad said Cam Mc Dorman farmed the area when in the 1930s and 40s, and outlines of fields and roads were still visible in the abandon land now covered with sprangletop grass. We'd rabbit and quail hunt in the abandoned mountain tier without much results, but it was good to be in the woods.

"Johnny, look at the hillside. Do you see anything?" Forster said, starting the training for a molly moocher gatherer.

"See what?"

"Keep looking." Then added a cue. "Look where the leaves are raised and disturbed."

On the shaded hillside, leaves were pushed up and the head of a sponge-like plant was protruding centered about the leave debris clutter. "Foster, is that one?"

"Johnny, you're on the way to become a 'merkel man!'" Forster slapped my shoulder saying, "Keep looking, I see at least three more."

Soon, I was a "merkel man" spotting the honeycomb like fungi lining the bottom of my paper bag with ten mushrooms. It was a good picking between the four mountain climbers, but Foster showed us up with his heavy bag of molly moochers.

"It looks like it a good haul of merkels, Foster," Mary, his wife, said when we emptied our bags on the back porch work table. "Just put them in the bucket of water. It's already been salted," she instructed. Mary would allow the mushroom to soak to insure bug free merkels while Foster relaxed on the front porch.

"Johnny, you've never had fired merkels?" Mary asked at the kitchen table with a platter of breaded fried merkels. I'm surprised you didn't get Oma to fry up a mess. I would have thought Ted would like molly moochers."

"Mary, merkels are the best!" I responded without trying to explain Ma Mow Oma's personal thoughts about working on the day of rest.

The summer before, Happy (Delmer) Nelson and I went frog gigging on Big Coal River on a Saturday night. Happy worked at the ARMCO Nellis mines before the Second War and volunteered to join the army, although he could have remained in the mines since it was considered strategic work and entitled coal miners to a deferment. Happy never returned to the mines after his honorable discharge, and worked in the community as a handy-man. Happy and his brother, Torr, had stormed the Normandy Beaches and fought in the Battle of the Bulge. Happy, like so many war-torn veterans that returned, never spoke of their war experiences. Once Happy become angry after listening to a kid brag about his father's experiences. Happy angrily said after the boy left, "Johnny, his father was well behind the lines cause no one on the lines talks about it!"

Nearly every Brushton household during the 1950s had family members that had served during the Second War, but war stories didn't abound. It was accepted that they had served and returned to their families: Pa Paw Ted, (Army, Europe), Uncle Reginald (Giggs) (Navy, Pacific), Roy Pauley (General Patton's 3rd Army, Europe), Elvin (Junior) Smith, Ray Hutchinson (Navy submarines), Uncle John L. Hudson (Army, Panama Canal Zone) Ed Racier (Air Force, China), Carlos Epling (Army), and Delmer (Happy) and Torr Nelson (Army, Europe).

The river was different during the night, with sounds more pronounced. Bull frogs lined the water's edge, calling to attract mates or doing a territorial maneuver. I had paddled our boat two miles upriver from Brushton to await our evening frog gigging trip. A miner's battery and lamp were often commandeered, but Dad had rigged a car headlight with a pipe handle. Alligator clips were attached to a car battery located in the floor of the boat.

"Johnny, sounds like a big frog across the river. I'll get us across. Now, get ready!" Happy instructed from the rear seat. The light, when shown into the frog's eyes, froze the frog in place until the sharp prongs of the gig pinned them to the mud bank. "Johnny, turn the light out. I hear someone coming down river." Happy warned.

"Happy what's wrong? I got my fishing licenses in my tackle box." I responded.

"Johnny, I don't make it to Danville to get mine!" Happy said in a hushed voice. We pulled close behind a log jam that protruded from the Brier Branch side and waited for the boat to pass.

"Catching anything?" Happy called out to the stranger passing midstream. The boater wasn't startled since our spotlight sent a reflected beacon of light up from the surface of the river. Everyone in Brushton recognized the tell-tell-sign of a reflected light on the river.

"Just jitter-bugging. Nothing biting!" Came the response from the dark.

Happy laughed and reasoned, "The bloke didn't have a licenses either!" Happy was the only person to use the term "bloke," perhaps the only indicator he had spent time in England during the war. Happy had told me a story when England, waiting for the invasion, he and his buddies went to a local bar and happened to make acquaintance with a British beauty, who was also familiar with a group of British infantrymen. One of the Brits took offence of the Yank's attention and confronted him. The Yank cold-cocked him and the assaulted man attempted to get back to his feet. Happy reported one of the Brit's friends warned, "Just as well stay on the floor, because the 'bloke' will just knock your ass back down!" Happy laughed while relaying his only shared wartime experience with me.

Happy enjoyed Falstaff Beer, since a quart was always handy, but likely it was a means of self-medication brought on by his war experience. Regardless, there was never a more generous or kind person in Brushton.

"Ma Maw, I've got frogs!" I announced, barrowing through the back door.

"Land's sake, Johnny. Its bedtime, and they be spoiled if not cleaned tonight." Tunsel Barker was an early-to-bed farmer, not bothered with staying up late watching TV or listening to the radio, so I was reduced to becoming a frog gutter.

The room directly behind Ma Maw's kitchen was equipped with a single-bowl porcelain sink mostly used for my chemical experiment when Santa made the mistake and placed a Gilbert chemistry set under the tree. Ma Maw Oma loved frog legs bettered than anything, but would have made a sacrificed of not eating them if cleaned on Sunday. Time was running out, and I started to clean the dozen frogs. I had watched Dad clean frogs for Ma Maw in an attempt of winning her favor, so I imitated his cleaning technique. The problem with frogs is, even when cut into, the front portion of their bodies wants to continue jumping and crawling around the room. Frogs were jumping from the porcelain sink racing towards the kitchen. It would have been a real surprise if Ma Maw had found the front half of a petrified frog under her bed during spring cleaning. I placed them in a salt water bath in the Frigidaire.

"Johnny, the frog legs fried up mighty fine," Ma Maw said, as she placed the platter on the kitchen table. "You going to have some?"

"Ma Maw, we always have fried chicken on Sunday!"

"Johnny, they taste just like chicken!" Ma Maw said, shocked someone wasn't interested in fried frog legs.

"There all yours!" I insisted at the same time not wanting to admit I gagged the whole time while gutting and chasing frogs.

"Well son, what are you going to eat? Ted and I are going to enjoy your and Happy's frog legs."

"Ma Maw, I'll just have a bologna sandwich."

Chapter 15
Dropline Surprise

"Johnny, let's go check our lines. It's getting late, and I'll fall asleep in the boat," Larry grumbled.

"OK! I just want to finish the movie! Just ten more minutes," I argued.

"Johnny, we've seen "The Creature from the Black Lagoon" a thousand times, and it hasn't changed any! I want to get to bed!"

"Alright. But the longer we let the lines wait, the more fish we'll haul in," I countered in hopes of finishing the movie.

"I don't know why you want more fish! You can hardly stand to gut them, let along eat them."

"Now Larry, you know that not true!" I defended, taking offense that he would mention I had a weak stomach when it came to gutting fish.

"Well then Johnny, what did we do with last week's catch? You cleaned all of them, huh?"

"Larry, Sister Justice was so happy to get a load of catfish! You heard it yourself when she said, 'Cleveland was just saying he would love to have a plate of fried catfish.'" I said, offering a counter argument.

"Mrs. Justice was sure happy getting a load of fish, but I think you liked it better not having to gut them!" Larry and I made good fishing in Big Coal River between using a trotline strung across the river just below the "Big Rock," a favorite swimming hole at Brushton, and drop lines hung from low-hanging branches. "Mrs. Justice is sure a fish gutter. She is a fish cleaning machine!" Dad had as weak a stomach as me when it came to cleaning fish and when faced with a load of fish, he suggested taking them to Mrs. Justice. He had used her before as a ready and willing disposal for uncleaned fish. Dad had known the Justices for his entire life and always called them Mr. and Mrs. Justice, and Larry followed Dad's practice. I had a different relationship with the couple; they were Pilgrims with Ma Maw and Pa Paw, and I always addressed them as, Brother and Sister Justice.

"John Edward, you and the boys are a blessing, bring fresh fish for Cleveland and me. I'll have to tell Sister Jordan what a fine family she has raised." She continued to talk while gutting fish. When Dad laid out our catch, she didn't hesitate and jumped into the job. Dad was at ease talking to Sister Justice, much different than if talking to Ma Maw Oma, who would have turned a fish gutting into a sermon of five loaves of bread and two fish, rather than simply offering a word of thanks.

The Justices often held Wednesday night pray meeting at their home. I was allowed to wonder throughout their house. Over the living room fireplace an oil painting hung. I asked Sister Justice about it. She held a strong faith and was able to tell me about the memorial painting without losing composure. The painting was of Big Coal River above Brushton where their son, Aubrey, had drown. His fishing boat capsized during high water and was swept down river by the current, where he grabbed onto a tree extended above the river's floodplain. He panicked holding onto the tree with a death grip.

Sister Justice said that several men took boats to the stranded boy but were unable to loosen his hold, since recently he broke his arm and was in a cast. A crowd gathered on the train track above the river and helplessly watched as the rising water covered his head. Brother and Sister Justice's faith sustained them to be reunited with their son in the end. Grandpa and Grandma Hudson also lost a young son, Marion, when he hooked a large fish while fishing at the Big Rock and was pulled into the river.

Dad had spent his youth playing and fishing on Big Coal River and believed Larry and I were entitled to the same pleasure. A twelve-foot Sears' V bottom aluminum boat and a two-and-a-half horsepower boat motor were given to Larry and me. In places, the river was so shallow the propellers would extend into sandy river bottom and leave a trail similar to tracks of river mussels. "Johnny, do you have the bait can?" Larry asked as we made our way down the steep riverbank.

"Yes, do you think this is my first time running the lines?" I answered sarcastically.

"It would be near your first time gutting fish if you do the cleaning tomorrow," Larry countered.

"Larry, I'm no fish gutter! I'm a lover!"

Larry replied repeating our often repeated reference to one of Dad's fishing buddy's response when he fell for the tenth time on slick rocks while hunting lizards. "I'm no lizard hunter! I'm a lover!" We both laughed still not quite knowing the true meaning of the comeback phrase.

"Larry, you hear all that racket?" I warned as we made our way to the raised sandbank where our boat was tied. We fished during the summer, mostly catching mudcats and a few blue and channel cats, and an occasional bass with a casting rig. Dad bragged that Big Coal River, before he was a boy, was judged one of the best fishing rivers in the state, but toxic mine run-off and heavy silting as a result of clear-cut timbering, drift mines, and strip mining had reduced our fish haul to catfish. Larry and I did catch a monster mudcat that I persuaded our neighbor, Tunsel Barker, to gut and clean, and Ma Maw Oma fried it for dinner. Larry and I had a better record of water snake kills than fish catches; every flat rocks along the shoals below the Turnhole, was home to a family of water snakes. "Larry don't be scared, put your finger under the rock and flip it over! I've got a hand full of rocks ready to pound any snake." I often reassured him during snake hunting trips. Larry flipped the rock and retreated to retrieve throwing rocks he had stationed before the assault. The population of water snakes never decreased, unlike game fish.

"We must have another big mudcat on line!" Larry said excitedly. "Is Tunsel going to have to clean this one?" my brother teased.

"Larry, I did Tunsel a favor. He took the fish skin, its head, and the guts and buried them in his tomato patch just like the Pilgrims did."

"Do you think his tomatoes taste like fish guts?" Larry puzzled.

"I don't know anything about taste, but he said not to tell anyone his secret for big tomatoes, and you'll have to swear on Ma Maw's Bible not to tell Tunsel's secret."

"It's going to be hard to use Ma Maw's Bible since it's always in her hand."

"Larry, stop fooling! We've got a monster catfish!" I instructed as we pushed off from the Brushton side of Big Coal River. "Our picture will be in the Coal Valley News with this monster catch!" The willow tree's limbs were splashing against the water's surface and thrashing Larry and I taking a Lucille "switching."

"Hold the flashlight! I'll pull up our monster!" I pulled against the cotton twine to lift our prize into the boat. Within seconds of dumping our record catch, the #2 fish hook straightened, and Larry was thrown off balance and dropped our only flashlight into the river. I fell back with the release and screamed at Larry. "We need the light. What happened?"

"Larry was fast to respond, "You won't bring that Monster turtle from the Black Lagoon into the boat with me!"

Larry was traumatized, and described our catch as the largest turtle he had ever seen. "Johnny, that turtle was bigger than the turtle at Camden Park!" We continued to check our lines and pulled in catfish. Dad had fabricated a fish cage we used until we could clean the fish.

"Do you think Tunsel would have cleaned the monster turtle?" Larry asked, wondering how I was going to get the fish gutted and cleaned on a Sunday since Ma Maw Oma wouldn't consider frying Sunday-cleaned fish.

"Larry, I'm no fish gutter, I'm…." He stopped me from finishing our standard response.

"I don't know nothing about being a lover, but I know I'm not going swimming at the Big Rock until that monster turtle leaves town!"

"Never fear, when I am near!" I responded with our second favorite comeback failed. Dad first used the phrase to Uncle Dailey while traveling to Pocahontas County to deer hunt, and ran out of gas half-way between Droop and Marlinton.

"Johnny, you wouldn't be bragging if our snapper had got hold of you!" Larry teased. "I remember when you nearly drown when a little snake got on you!" he continued.

"Larry, you know that snake was eight-feet long!" I countered. "I don't know why you remember such insignificant things!" I attempted to defend my honor. It all started when Pergy Smith asked me what I wanted for my old JC Higgins bicycle. No one had money, so Pergy suggest a trade. I have no real attachment to the old bike, and Dad had a habit of making trades, and this made trading a hand-me-down skill.

"Percy, what do you have to trade?" I inquired.

"Johnny, I have two rabbits and a cage I'd be willing to trade." The Smith family lived up Brier Branch, Pergy, his sister, and a younger brother walked three-miles each way to the Brushton bus stop. Pergy was likely looking for transportation.

I had had cats and dogs as pets, but the idea of pet rabbits hit my fancy. "Pergy, I'll make the trade." Pergy took the bike and returned that evening with a cage containing two rabbits strapped to the rear fender.

"Ma Maw, look what I got." Then I added, "two rabbits."

"Land's sake, Johnny! We don't want rabbits. Mommy had rabbits, and they made a bigger mess than chickens!" She pointed her finger towards the back door. "Those rabbits are going back to Brier Branch in the morning!"

"Yes, Ma Maw." No one argued or tried to reason with her after she pointed her finger. I got word to Pergy: "The rabbits had to go!"

Pergy returned to Brushton and handed me a fly fishing rod and reel. I had heard about fly fishing and readily accepted the trade. Dad schooled me on technique, and I borrowed his old rubber fishing waders for a Saturday fishing trip.

Larry and I went upriver, and I waded into the rushing water of the shoals. "Larry, I'm sure to pull a bass with my new fish rod and reel," I bragged.

"You haven't caught anything yet," He yelled from the rocky floodplain.

"Dad said to be careful in waders," Larry repeated Dad's warning. "He was pulled under when he slipped."

"Larry!" I started to explain. "I've hooked a fish! I told you so." Bad things happen in threes. Over the sound of rushing river water, a ruckus was heard coming down the steep bank. I spotted a massive snake coming down, knocking loose rocks as it moved. "Larry!" I called in a panic. "Look at that snake. Throw some rocks so it will do downriver. I have a fish on my line." I had a flashing memory of Pa Paw's tale of hoop snakes rolling down hillsides ready to spring into an arrow and sting their prey with their poison tail. "Larry, it's a hoop snake! Throw some rocks!"

"Johnny, I can't throw that far!" Get out of the river!" Then added, "The snake coming directly at you!"

My fish was still online, and the snake stopped at the water's edge, slipping into the water. Water snakes swim both on top of the water and below the water's surface; usually when frighten they retreat underwater, where they swim much faster. The snake slipped into the water and kept its head above water coming at a fast pace directly at me as if on attack.

"Johnny get out of the water." Larry screamed, "It's coming at you!"

I started to back up, keeping an eye on the fast-approaching, whose mouth was now wide open. I slipped, and, fell into the cold water, and as Dad had warned, the waders filled with water dragging me down river. My feet found support on a submerged rock and I was able to stop my downriver movement, but the enormous snake was nearly on top of me. My only weapon was my new fly rod and reel, and I started whipping at the open mouthed snake with the rod.

"Larry! Larry!" I called to my brother, but he was disabled with laugher.

I regained my footing and made way to the safety of the rocky riverbank. Larry was still dying with laughter but regained his composure long enough to say, "You sure are a mighty-fine fly fisherman, Johnny!" and then added, "You ready to give it another try?"

I stood there with just the cork rod handle and the

reel in hand. I lost my hooked fish, lost my new rod, and nearly drown pulled down by flooded waders with a rabbit snake doing it best to put its stinger into me.

"Thanks for all your help, Larry!" I angrily reprimanded.

"Thank you, Johnny for the greatest fish story! I can't wait to tell Dad about your fly fishing skills," he finished and started to gather his gear.

"Larry, no one need to know about this; besides no one going to believe you!" I warned.

"Doesn't matter. Everybody knows if there's a mishap, you're in the middle of it!"

"You think Pergy will trade back my bike?" I commented.

"I don't think it came with a guarantee!"

Homemade Flies

Purple eyes, homemade flies.
Sliver sides, like a water bug glides.
A riverbank sight, Sliver of light.
Shimmering, glimmering bright.
Calling, calling for a fish to fight.

Purple eyes, homemade flies.
Complex ties, resting on the rise.
Angler's aim, never the same.
Whipping, dipping, lashing lure.
Casting, casting, dancing towards shore.
Splashing, dashing, searching for more.

Purple eyes, homemade flies.
Wings a flight, dragonflies a light.
Stepping stone circles, fly in flight.
Singing, sinking, prancing towards shore.
Graceful water bird, fancy dancing lure.

Purple eyes, homemade flies.
Practice perfect, countless tries.
Waterproof beetle, taken bait.
Reeling, pulling, what a fight.
Running, cunning, clever fish.
Every angler's wish.
Open krill, trophy trout
What a thrill, looking, seeking.
Homemade flies, with purple eyes.

Chapter 16
Peytona Beach

"Johnny, are you sure you need spats? You have both short and long pants and shirts, a neckerchief and slide, long and short socks, and a hat. But spats?" Mom asked while checking off items on her list while we stood at the checkout counter in the Scout department at the Diamond Department Store in Charleston.

"Mom, the picture in the Scout Book shows spats; its official." I replied. My interest in spats came from Uncle Red, Ma Maw's older brother, who had a bad ankle and wore gray wool spats for support and to keep his ankle warm. He was dapper, and it was a chance for me to have my own army green spats.

It was like Christmas, I also received official nylon swimming trunks, a sleeping cot, sleeping bag, mess kit, and an official Scout knife and hatchet. I modeled my new wardrobe for Mom and Ma Maw when we returned home.

The Nellis Troup 287 had been reinstated and we Scouts were anxious to take our first overnight camping trip to Peytona Beach. The beach was the premier recreational site on Big Coal River, with flat sandy beaches on both sides of the river. The beach was used for everything from swimming to baptism, from family picnics to a place for late night clandestine encounters. Unlike most of Coal River, the water was deep from one side to the other and the sandy beach was of white quartz with small dot of black coal particles either caused by eons of mountain erosion or spoils from mine operators' practice of draining impounded waste pits of sludge produced from the process of cleaning mined coal. Whenever there was a nighttime release, the river would run black for a day, often it appeared thick enough to walk upon, and it was a mystery how aquatic life could survive the midnight release of the black flood.

Jerry Hudson, Uncle Red's son, was the driving force behind the reinstatement of Troop 287. Ed Racer, Hillary Kinder, Carlos Epling, and Mr. Abbott joined together to develop an outstanding organization for our community.

"Pick up firewood by the riverbank," one of the leaders instructed. "You'll be cooking your own dinner," came follow-up encouragement. Much of the river bank had been picked over, but the supply of firewood was replenished with every high water. While swimming, one scout lucked upon a deposit of lump coal. The soft coal was rounded by erosion but wasn't a good indicator of time in the river, unlike the rough-edged sandstone that laid along the river. The scattered coal could have resulted in overspill from river barges that had not traveled the Coal River Navigation Canal since 1916 or the bottom refuge of impoundment ponds that had escaped preparation plants. In combination with drift wood, the rounded coal burned, releasing the near-forgotten smell of train steam engines and Nellis fireplaces.

An early morning heavy fog settled on the beach leaving my new sleeping bad cold and wet. Late morning, the camp fires were drowned with river water, and we returned home. The damp sleeping bag was hung over the clothesline and Ma Maw warmed a last breakfast she held in the oven.

Chapter 17
When I First Saw Beauty

"Everyone has a different idea of what beauty looks like to them," Mrs. Opal Dale Evans, the Nellis Elementary fifth grade reading teacher, suggested. "Some see beauty in a church building, and others may see beauty in a blue sky. Make a list of five things you think are beautiful." She ended her instructions, believing it should be an easy assignment and one that would generate discussion. Nellis school had instituted departmentalizing, and Mrs. Evans, a recent graduate of the University of Virginia (Charlottesville) in English-language arts (ELA), was an ideal teacher for students that had endured classes of students taking turns of oral reading. Encouraging students to take ownership of topics for discussion was a new teaching technique she instituted.

"Mrs. Evans?" Jimmy Stuart said as he raised his hand. "I don't think what I see as beautiful will be the same as what you want."

"Jimmy, everyone has a different idea of beauty, and what I may think, may be different than what you believe to be a thing of beauty." The teacher noted that several students were hesitant to make their list. Beauty is an abstract concept, and students were unpracticed in expressing their ideas for fear of being wrong, or worse, of being embarrassed. "Let me give you some example of what people may see as beauty." She didn't want to rush into the abstract, but offered a list of acceptable objects. "Flowers along the roadside, a pretty girl, or a newborn baby." She waited for the suggested objects to be absorbed.

"What I think of isn't sweet like a baby!" Jimmy replied.

"Well, Jimmy, we won't laugh. What is beautiful to you?" she said, hoping to start the discussion. Then gave a warning to the class and a reassurance to Jimmy. "No one is to laugh or make fun of Jimmy's idea of beauty, because everyone is getting a turn and your idea may be strange to some."

"A dead rabbit!" he replied. The seasoned teacher stood to practice the classroom management technique of proximity.

The classroom, although stunned, remained civil to their classmate and his odd concept of beauty. "Tell us more, Jimmy!" the teacher said to encourage discussion.

"Everyone's going to make fun!" he protested.

"Jimmy, there's a lot of famous painting hanging in museums of dead rabbits hanging by their legs. Someone else saw beauty in dead rabbits!" Mrs. Evans encouraged and thinking ahead to bring an art book of dead rabbits. "Some artists have even painted cows as a thing of beauty."

"Cow! Smelly cows?" Connie Woods questioned.

"Yes even smelly cows!"

"I like dead rabbits, because it means we'll have rabbit for dinner. I love rabbit stew!" No one picked at families having a hard time. With mine closure and automation, many men that had worked their entire lives where now unemployed, and the Stuart family was at a greater disadvantage, since Mr. Stuart had been disabled in a mine accident. The family relied on the USDA Commodity Food Program for basic food needs of powdered eggs, powdered milk, and blocks of cheese. Jimmy and his brothers were regulars in the lunch line when seconds were served, and if they spotted someone not eating their serving of macaroni and cheese, the unwanted portion was scrapped into a Stuart's lunch tray.

Jimmy example eased the fear of being wrong, because there were no wrong answers. The master teacher planned to return to the concept of what is beauty building on the abstract concept of a beautiful personality or a beautiful spirit.

"Mrs. Evans, what do you see as beauty?" Connie inquired.

"You're going laugh!" she teased.

"Tell us, it's can't be as bad as a dead rabbit!" Jimmy interjected.

"All right. But you promised not to laugh." She timed her response, allowing all attention to be dawned to her idea of beauty. "When you drive up Brush Creek and pass the Morning Star Baptist Church and look upon the hillside, the mixture of pink, red, white, and black is breath taking. The colors are like a master's painting!"

Jimmy was the first to respond. "Mrs. Evans, you mean the Ridgeview slate dump?"

"Yes. It is a work of beauty!" She looked to the window like she was viewing the slate dump to add dramatic emphasis.

The classroom erupted in laughter. "Mrs. Evans, that's the slate dump! Its smoke burns your eyes, and nothing lives in Brush Creek after it runs pass the dump!" Tena Smith added.

"Maybe so, but the blend of pink and red with a splash of white and black is spectacular, a thing of beauty," she concluded, confident she had stimulated discussion beyond the classroom.

"Can you believe Mrs. Evans is in love with the stinky Ridgeview slate dump?" Tena joked.

I was as shocked as the classroom with Mrs. Evans revelation. "Ma Maw, do you think the Ridgeview slate dump is a thing of beauty?" I asked at dinner.

"Land's sake, Johnny. I never thought about it!" I failed to encourage additional comments, since she was talking about her mother's quilting party.

Grandma Hudson was a frugal Methodist and although they talked little of the Great Depression of the 1930s, one would think she was still trying to make ends meet. The family didn't have a great fortune but was blessed compared to most in Brushton.

"Ted, Mommy's got her quilting rack set up in her dining room. It took her, Mrs. Fleaner, and Aunt Ulla to push the dining room table against the wall," she informed Pa Paw and me.

"Oma, it's better than peeling apples in hot canning room in the middle of July!" Pa Paw said, trying to calm his wife.

"They all love their quilts! I told Mommy we could buy new blankets at Sears. I thought she was going to have a stroke!"

"Oma, our quilts are a thing of beauty! I couldn't sleep at night not covered with one of our quilts. Next to apple butter, it's a blessing to everyone to get one of our quilts for Christmas."

"Ma Maw, I'd rather have a quilt than apple butter," I said, still thinking of Mrs. Evans' slate dump confession.

"Johnny, you love Grandma's apple butter! Can I get you a spoon full of apple butter for your biscuit?" Pa Paw teased, knowing that Old Gyp helped me with apple buttered toast.

Grandma Hudson's quilts were made of leftover scraps of material and old dresses sown into twelve-inch pattered blocks that would be placed on a cotton backing made from salvaged hundred-pound flour sacks. Hudson's Big Star, although a modern self-service full line grocery store, still catered to the needs of country people. Families continued to made homemade biscuits, and for large families, a hundred pounds of flour was a monthly purchase. I once asked a country cook why she used so much flour, and she told me she made biscuits and gravy for her husband's hunting dogs since dog food was so expensive. The flour sacks would be cut at their seams and bleached to remove the printing on the sack. The old ladies would work, piecing the quilt with a layer of cotton batting in the center, giving the quilts body and warmth.

"Johnny, we're going to Madison. I need to stop at the bank," Mom informed me as we headed up Brush Creek. We passed through Nellis and on to Ridgeview. On the left side of the valley, behind the Morning Star Baptist Church and before passing under the Ridgeview coal tipple, I looked at the blended colors of red-dog, and recognized what Mrs. Evans was talking about. The first time I saw "beauty."

I saw beauty in the Ridgeview slate dump, while Grandma Hudson and her old lady friends saw beauty in flour sack quilts and apple butter; Ma Maw Oma saw beauty in the Pilgrim community and fried chicken; and Pa Paw saw beauty in his family and telling stories to his grandson, Johnny.

Chapter 18
Last Wake at Bloomingrose

The front parlor was unlocked, allowing a rare glimpse inside the room that always felt cold. It was a twin to the living room with a back-to-back coal burning fireplace in the center wall, now sealed, and replaced with a gas space heater. The fireplace mantle was fancier than the others, adorned with a gilded mirror against a 1940s pink floral wallpaper, and a collection of curios that held special meaning only to Aunt Lydia. The room had served for the final above-ground site for bereavement for the Midkiff family for over sixty years. The old great-grandparents likely were the first, followed by Grandpa George, then two deceased brother, Raymond and Joel, then Other Mon, and now, my Grandpa James, Mom's father.

The custom of waking a loved one in the family's home wasn't considered an exception but a practical solution for families limited by available funeral parlors or limited funds. Often, the funeral service was performed at church followed by a grave-side final farewells and a prayer. The casket was positioned against the upriver double windows, open for viewing, and a final photo was taken since so few photo were available of Grandpa James. The room was small, but at the time a large room compared to other local homes, and had several straight back chairs and a 1940s-style davenport. Friends came to show respect then moved through the large farmhouse, visiting with friends and family. Wakes and funerals served as re-acquaintance opportunities for the community and family as the friendly gathering often served to ease the pain of death.

"Thank you for coming Earl, James was a great supporter of yours." Aunt Lydia greeted Sheriff Earl Miller in the front parlor. Local politicians depended on leading county families' support to gain office, and like all county elected offices, once elected, it was an office held for life, inconvenienced every four-years by an onslaught of handshaking and baby kissing. Aunt Lydia was the self-appointed family matriarch, earned by her residency in the family's home, her positions as a principal at Seth Elementary, her control over family assets, or, as some suggested, her dominating personality.

"Miss Midkiff, James was a good friend; he will be missed." The politician spilled out the well-worn phrase. It wasn't considered judgmental to address the 62-year-old Lydia Midkiff as "Miss"; it was the accepted practice. Some disgruntle relatives whispered, she once had a love, and he died from injecting taunted moonshine. I failed to ask Aunt Lydia of her dead lover, but I would suspect she would have responded, to the surprising question, similar to when I told her I was going to kick her eyes out with my pointed-toed boots from Oklahoma. "Johnny, that doesn't sound like you!" Likely, followed by a next door confrontation with Uncle George: "George, what sort of foolishness are you telling the boy? Just sounds like mean talk to me!"

The sheriff moved towards Grandma Edna to offer condolences. "Mrs. Midkiff, your husband was a good friend, he will be missed."

Grandma stood and responded, "Earl, thank you for coming. James thought highly of you and your family." Then took her seat readied to accept other well-wishers. The politician moved to the living room to greet other mourners with a hand shake and back slap. In the dining room, the table had an array of food, from deviled eggs to sliced ham. Several Church of Christ women worked from the kitchen to replenish emptied platters. It wasn't a big gathering of mourners since most would attend the next-day funeral service.

Grandpa Midkiff had been sickly for the last year, and Mom visited him at the hospital the previous weekend. She had so hoped her father could have seem his newest granddaughter, my sister, Nioka Michelle Jordan, born a month before. He was fascinated with her name crediting it to a Native American name, but she was named by Dad for Nyoka, The Jungle Girl, after viewing and falling in love with the jungle girl at the Nellis Theater in 1941.

"Johnny, you and Larry stay close." Followed by, "You're not to go upstairs!" I was disappointed when I saw Aunt Lydia had padlocked the door going upstairs. "No one needs to chase after you all!" Mom instructed as she worked to greet family and friends that came to show respect. Home wakes were rapidly becoming a past practice, but Grandpa Midkiff's funeral service was the exception and conducted at the Midkiff home. Perhaps it was a last request or just following family tradition, but other family services were at the Bloomingrose Church of Christ.

"Yes, Mom. Don't worry!" I reassured Mom as we pulled towards the back door. Smokers had gathered in the sunporch, decorated with Aunt Lydia's only indoors plants, violets, by the back door, while food continued to travel from the kitchen to the dining room table. Larry and I made our way to the back yard to visit with the chickens and pigs. Old Daisy was gone, and the Midkiff family was forced to eat Chiffon margarine. Chickens still came to the fence, hoping for a handful of feed, and the pigs rooted at their trough, hoping for a spillage of Seth Elementary kitchen slop. The one lone June apple tree was leafless, but ready for a spring burst of white flowers. The garden was untilled despite Grandpa's superstition that insured a good crop of always planting potatoes on St. Patrick's Day, the week before the service. The March day was warm under a sky blue, but the Bloomingrose farm was quickly changing.

"Larry, you think you can hit the old car from here?" I asked while looking for a new target to throw clods of clay at. Unattended boys always resort to throwing rocks. If we were at the river's edge we skipped rocks, on the hillside above the C&O railroad we rolled rocks down the mountainside to bang against the sides of coal cars; rock throwing was in our blood and a way of life. Once we targeted Aunt Lydia's pigs with a barrage of rocks, the pigs retaliated and nearly came across their makeshift fence. Pigs were replaced as target with chickens, and Aunt Lydia complained her chickens had stopped laying eggs. The old 1938 black Dodge rested when it broke down before I was born, fronted the pig's pen.

"No problem." Larry let go of a high flying clod of clay that centered the driver's side of the divided windshield.

"Good shot!" I screamed excited Larry had zeroed in on target. I followed with several shots and soon the car's windows were reduced to hanging shattered glass, and we returned to Aunt Lydia's house.

The Bloomingrose Church of Christ choir waited on the front yard for Mr. Cantley's pitch tuner signal. The immediate family along with the preacher remained in the front pallor, and family and guests were seated along the front porch and in folding chairs supplied by the Johnson Funeral Home. The front door remained open and the front single window was open, allowing the preacher's eulogy to escape and the voices of the choir to enter the front parlor. Dad stood by Mom and she weep.

The preacher finished, the pitch turner unified the tone of the final hymn, a red rose was taken as a remembrance to later be pressed into the family Bible, and the pallbearers carried the casket through the door onto the Midkiff homestead's front porch. Heads were bowed in respect, last tears were shed, and the unified voice of the Bloomingrose Church of Christ choir offered final comfort to family and friends. The slow walk procession passed by the side yard flower garden, as the lock turned on the front parlor door for the last time.

Soon afterwards, spring flowers bloomed in the side yard garden, and June apples covered the hard-pack clay ground where honey bees and yellow jacket worked the fallen fruit, but time had caught up at the Bloomingrose farm.

Biography

I grew up in the southern coalfields of West Virginia, where the mountain culture nurtured a closeness of family. I spent my childhood sitting on a front porch on a Sunday afternoon listening to old folks talk about times past. The stories centered on their life experiences growing up in the mountains, surviving the Great Depression, hunting trips, snow storms, and great river floods. My grandfather, Edward Lee Jordan (Ted), entertained me with stories growing up at Hernshaw when the country was still a vast, virgin forest. The weekly return trip to our home at Brushton, West Virginia, from White Sulphur Spring, where we lived while Dad, his father, and brother worked on the secret bomb shelter at the Greenbrier Hotel allowed my brother, Larry Allan Jordan, my sister, Michelle Jordan Halstead, and me to listen to Dad's stories of his boyhood growing up during the Great Depression and World War II. My grandfather and Dad taught me the art and practice of storytelling that is unattainable in academic settings.

Our mother, Lucille Midkiff Jordan, was the backbone of my elementary and secondary education; yet I owe an enormous debt to Boone County teachers. I earned a bachelor's degree in Criminal Justice with majors in history, political science, and sociology from West Virginia State College. I credit State with providing me with an expansive view and understanding of the world gained by time spent in study with many of my instructors who were of the highest academic caliber.

While working at a grocery store at Racine, West Virginia, I met the woman who changed this country boy's main focus from making sure that every dollar that passed through Racine traveled at least once through his hands. When I first saw her come into the store, I mentioned to one of the carry-out boys, "That is someone I would like to marry." He laughed and said that she was too skinny.

Marian Ruth Walton graduated from the University of Hawaii and was in search of a teaching assignment in special education. On the bulletin board at her university, she noticed a posting for special education jobs in Boone County, West Virginia, and she came to Peytona Elementary just down the road from my work. In 1977 we were married in a double ceremony, along with Marian's younger sister, Diana Grey, and her husband, Scott, at St. Francis Xavier's in Metairie, Louisiana, and later made our home in Slidell, Louisiana.

I felt we would live in Slidell for only a short time while I worked with my father-in-law at his automotive wholesale company, John M. Walton Inc., in New Orleans, Louisiana. The job offered me an outstanding opportunity to travel throughout Louisiana, Mississippi, and southern Alabama. I listened to many stories. Much of southern culture depends on storytelling, and it was like listening to my father and grandfather. It was truly a crucial influence in my development as a storyteller.

After the Walton family's business closed, I decided I wanted to become a social studies teacher—a career I had always wanted to pursue. I attended Southeastern Louisiana University at Hammond, Louisiana, working towards a master's degree in special education. Later, I worked on additional certification at Southern University at New Orleans.

All of my lifetime accomplishments pale in comparison to the success of my family. Marian and I have been married for 38 years and have five children: Our oldest, Trece Jordan-Larsen, is married to Brian with five children, Sarah, Laura, Julia, Gage, and Cayleigh and two granddaughters, Violet and Lena. Our second child, John Walton Jordan, is married to Paige White with one daughter, Genevieve and son, John Harrison. Our third and fourth children, Lee Walton Jordan and David Walton Jordan live in the New Orleans area working in the oil industry. Our fifth child, Logan Walton Jordan, is married to Alyssa Markham and has a son, Logan Jr. Our family was blessed when we shared our home with two foster children through Catholic Charities in New Orleans, Sammie and TaRoy, who are both now deceased.

I attribute my success to support and encouragement from Marian and our family.

Made in the USA
San Bernardino, CA
20 March 2016